Contents

I0080920

Terms used

We have attempted to use terms which keep the person central to our thinking and work and do not imply a particular framework of understanding. We have referred to experiences, behaviours and difficulties rather than symptoms of illness. The terms 'client' and 'service user' are both commonly used by practitioner psychologists, and although both are subject to debate, they are used here on occasion. We have tried to avoid labelling people, and hence refer to people with hoarding difficulties, rather than using the terms 'hoarder' or 'patient'.

We have included descriptions of what it's like to have difficulties with hoarding from people expert through experience. Some have chosen to use their own names, and some have chosen a pseudonym (indicated with an asterisk in the list of contributors), some prefer to remain anonymous.

Executive summary

This document provides information, guidance and recommendations for people working with those with hoarding difficulties. It is intended to be read by practitioner psychologists, and other psychological professionals, and used as a resource by those working both within NHS, social care and/or independently.

It provides information on what hoarding is, and the evidence for psychological intervention. It provides advice about management and care for those working with people with hoarding difficulties and for those planning and leading services.

WHAT IS HOARDING?

Hoarding is now being recognised as a distinct mental health difficulty of its own, with specific issues affecting access to services and psychological intervention. Hoarding can have a huge impact on a person's ability to function independently and can carry a high level of risk for themselves and others. It can cause high levels of distress for those sharing a home with or living close to the person who hoards, and can cause difficulties for communities working with people who hoard.

RECOMMENDATIONS

1. Mental health and social care services should provide services for people with hoarding difficulties regardless of how they access services.

2. Everybody already working with people who hoard should have access to training and information about good practice to ensure competence in the assessment of and interventions for hoarding.

3. There should be increased availability of training for psychological therapists, non-psychological professionals and non-professionals working with hoarding so that practitioners are competent.

4. When assessing someone who has problems with hoarding, attention should be paid to any other mental health problem where help could be offered, physical health problems should also be assessed.

5. Safeguarding issues for the person or anyone else who lives in the property need to be considered.

6. Practitioner psychologists should advocate for and be involved in the multiagency working approaches that have developed in the last ten years. Multiagency working is a vital part of the work for people with hoarding problems.

7. Interventions should be based on the best current evidence. The research evidence so far suggests that CBT is currently the primary psychological intervention, which can be individual or in groups.

8. An increase in research evidence is required to improve our understanding of phenomenology and the effectiveness of psychological intervention and support for hoarding for both individuals and the people living with or close to and affected by hoarding.

9. There is a need for national leadership on how hoarding is recorded. Currently there is no national reporting or consistent data coding. If people were asked to report centrally we would have a better record of needs and priorities for research and development of interventions.

10. The national media should seek advice from experts including practitioner psychologists about the portrayal of people with hoarding problems and continue the trend of not using mental health problems to entertain and shock the public as has been the case in the past.

> *The realisation that it was not just a clutter problem, it wasn't just me, was very significant. It was like an 'ah-ha' moment.*
>
> Christine

What is hoarding and how do we recognise it?

PART 1

Part 1: What is hoarding and how do we recognise it?

Key points

Hoarding difficulties are a combination of excessive acquisition of items, build-up of clutter and problems with disposal.

With a specific definition and identifiable characteristics, hoarding is recognised as an entity in its own right.

Hoarding difficulties have a relatively high prevalence in comparison with more familiar problems in which services intervene.

Hoarding is now recognised as a distinct mental health difficulty on its own rather than solely an aspect of obsessional compulsive difficulties or as a 'lifestyle choice'. Steketee et al. (2000) have developed and used a definition for many years but only now is hoarding included in DSM-5 as a discrete and separate disorder (APA, 2013). While there are debates about the usefulness of diagnosis (BPS, 2011), an acknowledgement of the very real and distinct difficulties associated with hoarding has been widely valued.

There are some very specific issues relevant for working with people who hoard that differ from other mental health problems. An acknowledgement of hoarding as a mental health problem allows for greater research evidence to develop, and an improved understanding of how we best help those struggling with it and those affected by it. In addition, many people with hoarding difficulties have been very gratified to see it recognised 'officially'.

A definition of hoarding

The World Health Organization in their most recent diagnostic manual, ICD-11, classified hoarding as a disorder, and this came into effect from January 2022. Their definition, reflects the views of clinicians and researchers, and is as follows:

> *'Hoarding disorder is characterised by accumulation of possessions due to excessive acquisition of or difficulty discarding possessions, regardless of their actual value. Excessive acquisition is characterized by repetitive urges or behaviours related to amassing or buying items. Difficulty discarding possessions is characterized by a perceived need to save items and distress associated with discarding them. Accumulation of possessions results in living spaces becoming cluttered to the point that their use or safety is compromised. The symptoms result in significant distress or significant impairment in personal, family, social, educational, occupational or other important areas of functioning.'*
>
> (WHO, 2019/2021).

> *I like to see it mount up sometimes ... because I think I can find another use for it.*
>
> Danielle

PEOPLE AND POSSESSIONS

Hoarding is a behaviour that is not confined to humans.

No other species, however, comes close to human beings in how we mediate our lives through objects. In understanding hoarding it is useful to keep in mind how people in general interact with their things, give value to them, use them to achieve things, demonstrate identity through them and become attached to them.

Can't have any one over syndrome – CHAOS. I wonder if part of me doesn't want to have any one over.

Harry

People develop attachments (and even intimacy) with inanimate objects:

> *We become attached to objects out of sentiment, perhaps, or for their symbolic value – a wedding ring, a grandmother's quilt, an old fountain pen – all of which may commemorate personal history. We seem to accept the idea that things have a life of their own. And that acceptance is the beginning of having an emotional relationship with inanimate objects... we seem to have developed a psychic intimacy with stuff.*

(Busch, 2004, pp.15–16).

The concept of possession of objects as if part of ourselves is established by the age of two.

In childhood, intense relationships can develop with one particular object to which the obvious term attachment object is ascribed. The term transitional object is also used as the object is seen to provide a role in gaining independence from parents. In the teenage years, possessions start to act as a crutch for the self (Jarrett, 2013). For instance, when children in the age range 8–18 years were asked 'What makes you happy?', they chose a material possession – a tendency which peaked in middle adolescence (Chaplin & John, 2007). At this time, possessions can increasingly become a reflection of who or what we are, and this continues into adulthood. Thus, our relationship with objects over our lifespan has a developmental progression.

Consumption of possessions, as a marker of social status, has been increasingly encouraged by the mass media since the 1950s. Objects collected may also convey messages about membership of a particular group.

> *Like a uniform, our possessions of specific objects and brands can also signal our membership of social groups, both to others and to ourselves.*

(Jarrett, 2013)

A football fan, for example, may collect everything they can that is related to their team.

In older life, our possessions take on an increased role as aide de memoires of the life that has been lived, as an aid to reflection, for nostalgia and also a source of comfort. Mostly, this is healthy and fits with a fulfilling ageing process. Our relationships with objects echo the framework of our relationships with people.

> *As with human relationships, the attachments to our things deepens with the passage of time. Elderly people (sic) are surrounded by possessions that have followed them through good times and bad.*

(Jarrett, 2013)

ACQUIRING POSSESSIONS – COLLECTING OR HOARDING?

Despite the seemingly simple developmental progression described above, it has long been recognised that people and their possessions have a complex relationship. In fact, the behavioural tendency to acquire and then retain possessions can be seen as operating on a continuum from normal/adaptive to that of excessive/ pathological (Pertusa et al., 2010). There is good evidence that collecting is a common feature of everyday life.

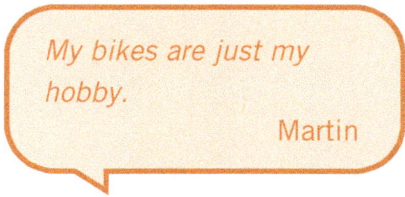

> My bikes are just my hobby.
>
> Martin

Prevalence estimates of collecting indicate that approximately one-third of the US and UK population have been collectors at some point (Pearce,1998) with collecting particularly common (91 per cent) in children aged 6–10 (Baker & Gentry, 1996).

There appear to be five key characteristics for collecting of tangible objects (Subkowski, 2006):

1. Behavioural search, selection and storage of possessions.

2. The collection being systematic and limited in a defined area.

3. Additional interest in the background to the collection (i.e. secondary information).

4. A marked affective component (i.e. having a 'passion' for the collection).

5. A fairly long-term behaviour.

It is possible to compare and contrast collecting with hoarding (Nordsletten & Mataix-Cols, 2012 – see Table 1). An interesting feature of collecting (like hoarding) is that it often entails building a collection of objects with relatively low economic value, with individual items being granted elevated, high personal value by the collector, due to their place and position in the collection (Pearce, 1998).

Table 1: Differences between people who self-identify as collectors and those who self-identify as hoarders

Hoarding	Collecting
Avoidance of discard	Discard by trading to improve collection
Widespread unstructured and excessive acquisition across object categories	Themed and structured limited acquisition in discernable category
High sense of responsibility and sentimentality	Lower sense of responsibility and sentimentality
Discard difficulties are long term	Discard difficulties fluctuate
Large physical size of the hoard	Small physical size of the collection
Disorganised and chaotic display (shame and humiliation)	Organised display (pleasure and pride)
High emotional distress	Low emotional distress
High social, occupational and relational impairment	Low social, occupational and relational impairment
No shared interest with others about the objects kept	Common shared interest with a group who also collect

For some people, who might be described by others as hoarders, for some their identity as a collector is very significant. Even when they are described by others as hoarders, they may not see themselves as having a problem with hoarding; their view is that they have run out of room for their collection. For some people, the acquisition of items may have initially begun as a collection, but gradually spiralled out of control.

People who collect are more likely to share their interest with others – 84 per cent of people who collect describe the sharing of their interest with others as important. Collectors tend to trade items, swap, use online market places and attend specialist fairs to acquire the 'missing' item from their collection. In contrast, people who hoard are much less likely to share their interest with others.

LIVING WITH POSSESSIONS

Another significant difference is in the ability to organise possessions in and around the home. People who collect, organise, clean and catalogue their things. They tend to be quite methodical in looking after their belongings. People who have difficulties with hoarding are unlikely to be organised about sorting and cataloguing. Collectors tend not to overwhelm their living space with possessions and this may be associated with their ability to manage and organise their possessions better. Another distinction is that collecting tends to decrease over a lifetime, a process described as steady disengagement, whereas difficulties with hoarding tend to increase with age.

Is the clutter around me a reflection of the confusion within?
Danielle

It is not known whether there is a distinct difference in the distress associated with disposal between people who hoard and people who collect. It seems likely that both groups would find disposal difficult and emotionally distressing. Both groups are likely to share a number of similar cognitions and thinking styles and have similar beliefs about the value of their belongings. In fact, there is often no difference in the objective value of items that are in a collection or in a hoard.

TRAUMA AND STRESSFUL LIFE EVENTS

People who hoard were found to not only be more likely to have experienced a traumatic event than those with OCD, but that the strongest association for trauma was with environmental clutter, rather than acquisition or discard difficulties (Cromer et al., 2007). Landau et al. (2011) were also able to show a higher rate of self-reported traumatic events amongst people who hoard than those with OCD, even after accounting for age, gender, education and depression.

Chia et al. (2021) systematically reviewed studies into early family environment and adverse and traumatic events, finding a complex pattern of relationship between insecure attachments, cold controlling families and adverse life events being related to the severity of hoarding. However, it was not possible to distinguish specific factors for hoarding compared to other clinical groups. The variability of studies and their small sample size means caution is needed in generalising from this review.

IS HOARDING PART OF OBSESSIVE COMPULSIVE DIFFICULTIES?

Hoarding was, until relatively recently, conceptualised as a feature associated with obsessive-compulsive disorder (OCD). However, evidence has now emerged of hoarding in the complete absence of any other aspects of OCD (Bloch et al., 2008; Samuels et al., 2008). The key differences between OCD and hoarding are presented in Table 2.

Therefore, although for the purposes of this document we recognise hoarding as a distinct entity, it should be borne in mind that hoarding may also be seen as co-occurring with OCD or related to OCD. Pertusa et al. (2008) defined similarities and differences between pure hoarding and hoarding as a dimension of OCD and these are presented in Table 3 to facilitate understanding.

Table 2: Key differences between OCD and hoarding (Mataix-Cols et al., 2010).

Hoarding	OCD
Cognitions about possessions do not typically trigger any compulsions to perform stereotyped rituals concerning the possession (e.g. a person who hoards would not feel the need to memorise any discarded item)	Cognitions typically trigger the compulsion to perform stereotyped rituals (e.g. the upsetting and intrusive obsessive thought about being a child sex offender triggers the compulsion to cancel the thought out via repeating a prayer continually)
Hoarding cognitions, beliefs and behaviours are experienced as ego syntonic (e.g. a hoarder would not perceive the collection and storage of objects found in a skip at all unusual)	OCD thoughts and behaviours are experienced as ego dystonic (e.g. the frequent washing associated with contamination obsessions are seen as illogical, but necessary)
Less likely to agree with others about the impact of their behaviour	Usually in agreement with others that their behaviour is causing difficulties

Table 3: Comparison of hoarding and OCD-related hoarding

	Hoarding	OCD-driven hoarding
Hoarding of common possessions and items	Yes	Yes
Hoarding of bizarre items (e.g. faeces and urine)	No	Yes
Why they hoard	The intrinsic (usefulness in the future) or sentimental (the feeling/memories attached) value	Range of obsessional themes
Hoarding triggered by obsessions	No	Yes
Presence of other OCD symptoms (e.g. symmetry obsessions)	No	Yes
Significant clutter in the home onset	Early 30s	Mid 20s
Ego syn/dystonic	Usually ego-syntonic	Usually ego-dystonic
Checking behaviours	Rare and mild	Frequent and severe
Obsessions related to hoarding	No	Yes
Internal (i.e. cognitive) compulsions	No	Yes
Impact on functioning	Typically moderate	Typically severe

CO-PRESENTING DIFFICULTIES

DEPRESSION AND ANXIETY

Frost et al. (2011a) have identified that depression is more common among people who hoard (42.9 per cent) than among those with OCD (21.9 per cent). This potentially has a significant impact on engagement with treatment, due to problems with motivation and/or problems concentrating on tasks agreed in or between sessions. Although Frost et al. (2011a) found no increase in anxiety difficulties, they found higher rates of social anxiety among men who hoard compared with men with OCD. Steketee and Frost (2014a) report that 25 per cent of people with hoarding difficulties have social anxiety.

POST-TRAUMATIC STRESS DISORDER (PTSD)

Overall rates of PTSD were no higher in people who hoard than in those with OCD, despite self-reported rates of trauma being higher in the hoarding group (nearly 50 per cent) (Frost et al., 2011a).

> *I think it's trauma... too many of them... loss, if you are dealing with loss it scrambles your brain.*
> Danielle

ATTENTION DEFICIT/HYPERACTIVITY

There is some evidence of an association between hoarding and attention deficit/hyperactivity disorder (Hartl et al., 2005) which is likely to increase the person's difficulties with distractibility and impulsive acquisition. Frank et al. (2014) found that children with hoarding problems had higher anxiety and were more commonly diagnosed with attention deficit hyperactivity disorder (ADHD). Hacker et al. (2012) studied children with a diagnosis of ADHD and found that those who also had hoarding difficulties were more likely to show inattentive and hyperactive/impulsive symptoms.

In a study of adults attending an outpatient clinic for ADHD, Morein-Zamir et al. (2021), found that they displayed an elevated level of hoarding symptoms linked to inattention, and suggested that people with ADHD should be routinely screened for hoarding problems. This is backed up by a recent study by Grassi et al. (2023), who compared people with a primary diagnosis of ADHD to people with a primary diagnosis of OCD, and found a co-occurrence of people who met the diagnosis of hoarding disorder of 32.1 per cent with ADHD and 8 per cent with OCD. The healthy control group had a rate of 4 per cent. Inattention and impulsivity are indicated as being partially predictive factors. Within the understanding of people with hoarding problems, as OCD's significance in relation to hoarding problems reduces, the importance of ADHD increases.

HOARDING AND PEOPLE WITH INTELLECTUAL AND DEVELOPMENTAL DISABILITIES

Research on hoarding by people with intellectual disabilities (ID) is limited. However, some children with ID engage in hoarding that is not linked to either OCD and/or autism (Testa et al., 2011).

To date, hoarding has been identified as part of the behavioural phenotype of only one specific ID syndrome, namely Prader-Willi Syndrome (PWS) (Storch et al., 2011a). The hoarding is very specifically related to the other phenotypic features of PWS and centres on hoarding food.

An important finding is that such behaviour is ego dystonic, leading to significant levels of distress in people with PWS (Dykens et al., 1996). The absence of any other associations between hoarding and other specific forms of ID suggests that, other than in PWS, instances of hoarding should be regarded as idiopathic and investigated as such. There is positive research evidence for effective interventions for people with intellectual disabilities who have hoarding problems, Kellett, Matuozzo & Kotecha. (2015) conducted CBT with 15 people with mild intellectual disabilities over six months; participants all completed, there were no adverse effects, and there were significant improvements in both environmental measures and self-report for a reduction in hoarding.

HOARDING AND AUTISM SPECTRUM CONDITIONS

Hoarding is particularly common in people with autism spectrum condition (ASC), both with and without intellectual disabilities, many of whom are estimated to collect material that is related to their special interest (South et al., 2005). However, the situation is complicated by the phenomenological overlap between hoarding and apparently similar behaviours associated with ASC. Similarly, this apparent overlap between ASC and hoarding has led to investigations of whether people whose primary difficulty is hoarding show more autistic traits than people with non-hoarding OCD. Such studies have identified that while people who hoard do show more autistic traits than the general population, there is no difference between people with hoarding and non-hoarding OCD (Pertusa et al., 2012). With regard to hoarding by people with ASC, the key issue is whether the behaviour is ego dystonic, as is the case in OCD, or ego syntonic, as is usually the case for the hoarding and collecting engaged in by people with ASC (Baron-Cohen, 1989). Other cases of hoarding by people with ASC may be related to issues of memory and identity: 'I collect therefore I am' (Skirrow et al., 2014).

> *Imagine that the physical laws under which the world operates were subject to sudden, random change... like objects sometimes fall downward and not at other times, fire may not always be hot. How could you function in such a world? I find that other people can be as baffling as that!*
>
> Harry

CHARACTERISTICS OF HOARDING DIFFICULTIES

AVOIDING DISCARD

Avoidance of discard and avoidance of thinking about discard are central maintaining aspects of hoarding (Kellett et al., 2010). Throwing things away in the rubbish, recycling or giving things to others can all be difficult for people that hoard. Often strong emotions can be triggered by attempts to discard, the person may fear that they will not be able to cope; this can lead to the person engaging in avoidance behaviours and putting off decision-making with no or limited discard occurring.

DEVELOPING CLUTTER

Having large amounts of possessions can creep up gradually over time. What may have started as a reasonable collection, can outgrow the space and increasingly become quite chaotic and disorganised. This can then lead to greater difficulty in knowing what is owned and where valued things are. As living space becomes increasingly compromised, organisation or sorting becomes more difficult; there simply isn't enough physical space to allow proper categorisation.

I struggle with tidiness… I often don't put things back where they belong after use.

Harry

EXCESSIVE ACQUISITION

Acquiring objects, items, and food is a behaviour that everyone engages in. As we develop our identity, and age, our acquisition behaviours change. We may begin by collecting interesting things, or stockpiling useful things, people may develop an identity as someone who re-uses, or recycles and become the recipient of others' unwanted items. Initially, the acquisition of objects may not itself cause difficulties, but coupled with lack of space and severe difficulties with discard, it can lead to a significant build up of possessions and significant associated impact on the home environment. People who hoard may also experience 'compulsive urges' to acquire things that others might consider lacking value, as well as having problems with compulsive buying. Examples might include things found in skips, rubbish bins or car boot sales.

If you handle it, it's very hard not to buy it.

Danielle

I find it extremely frustrating knowing I've got it but I can't find it.

Harry

DIGITAL POSSESSIONS

As we move further towards a digital world, hoarding is also being seen as associated with electronic information. People might find storage on hard drives begins to run out and buy large amounts of online storage or physical hard drives (Zerkel, 2014). This can lead to difficulties finding information, or reduce the ability of the computer to function, leading to further purchases. Difficulties associated with excessive acquisition can also apply to mobile phones – for instance, avoiding deleting apps from a smart phone can lead to the phone becoming slow and unresponsive (Ehrlich, 2012).

The point at which this becomes a real problem is when the person becomes unable to use their phone, or find their photos or information due to the overwhelming amount stored or the need to keep perfect records of everything.

Research into digital hoarding is relatively new. One of the first studies by Sweeton, Sillence and Neave (2018), comprised a qualitative study of 46 people, and they found similar themes to physical hoarding. People had problems with over-accumulation of digital materials, with anxiety relating to accumulation and difficulty deleting. McKellar et al. (2020), in a study of 20 people who scored highly on the Digital Hoarding Questionnaire, found four dimensions for digital hoarding: anxiety, disengagement, compliance and collection. Whomsley (2020) states that there is a need to research how to help and maintain good habits for children and adolescents in their relationship to digital media so that they do not become hoarders of it.

ANIMALS

The Hoarding of Animals Research Consortium (2013) gave the following criteria for identifying the hoarding of animals:

1. Having more than the typical number of companion animals.

2. Failing to provide even minimal standards of nutrition, sanitation, shelter and veterinary care.

3. Neglect often resulting in illness and death from starvation, spread of infectious disease and untreated injury/medical conditions.

4. Denial of the inability to provide this minimum care and the impact of that failure on the animals, the household and human occupants of the dwelling.

5. Persistence in accumulating and controlling animals.

People who hoard animals may have past attachment issues, so animals become substitutes for people. There may be complex grief and a need for love, affection and care (Nathanson & Patronek, 2012; Prato-Previde, Ricci & Colombo, 2022).

People who hoard tend to self-neglect themselves, and their animals, are often in denial of the situation and they no longer recognise neglect. Homes can become unsafe with floorboards soaked in ammonia from urine and faeces, be structurally unsound, and lack safe access and egress posing health risks for humans and animals. Further risks include bites, scratches and disease transfer from animal to human or animal to animal. Hoarded animals are often cats and dogs, but also reptiles and horses; any animal could be hoarded.

People who hoard animals rarely seek help themselves. Attention is drawn to hoarding animals when it becomes a problem for someone else: when it is considered an issue of public health, animal welfare or a nuisance.

These cases are usually complex, time consuming and challenging, with animal welfare issues adding extra moral and ethical dilemmas context. There is not a lot of evidence as to what works, but it seems a multidisciplinary approach offers most to utilise different skills: a vet to consider animal welfare, a social worker to consider humans. Professions that typically become involved include animal welfare organisations, mental health, social services, housing providers, environmental health, emergency services, health professionals, veterinaries, and voluntary services. Teams currently working on complex cases may be best placed with transferrable skills for working with these cases. Collaborative working relies on trust and the ability to share data. Enforced removal of animals does not work. A clean, clear, and move-forward approach is only likely to work in negotiation with the individual and if the issue with the person is addressed psychologically; failure to do so inevitably leads to hoarding animals again. The trust of the person hoarding animals will also have been lost and is difficult to regain.

Two approaches worth considering as having the potential to play a part in this area are those of Hill et al. (2019) and Williams, Harris and Gordon (2022). Hill et al. (2019) took a harm minimisation approach where she worked with multi-cat homes with a neutering approach that was negotiated with the cat owners to reduce colony size. Welfare scores were improved at two and twelve-month follow-ups. Williams, Harris and Gordon (2022) used a motivational interviewing approach to work with equine hoarding by training equine welfare officers in this approach.

The legislation that is important in addition to that relevant for physical hoarding, is the Animal Welfare Act 2006, sections 4 and 9, which cover 4 Unnecessary Suffering and 9 Animal Welfare ('5 Freedoms'). It is discretionary for local authorities to become involved with animal welfare. There is a cost to becoming involved in such cases, including housing and providing care for any animals removed. The RSPCA does much work in this area, but they do not have to get involved as they are a voluntary organisation, have no powers of entry and have to bring private prosecutions. They prefer not to bring prosecutions in these cases as they do not want to criminalise someone with a mental health problem.

In addition to issues about the welfare of the animals involved, there are also health and safety issues beyond those created by other forms of hoarding, for both the person hoarding and anyone visiting the property (Moran & Patterson, 2011).

Defining hoarding as a mental health problem

Hoarding is now included in DSM-5 (APA, 2013) as a discrete and separate disorder (see appendix A for further information. It is also included in ICD 11, 2019/21). There are mixed views about this among colleagues and from people/families struggling with hoarding. As practitioner psychologists, dealing with this tension is familiar (BPS, 2013a). We use a formulation-driven approach in our work, so diagnosis is a contentious theme. Without a diagnosis, there is a risk of people being wrongly excluded from services because their difficulties are not recognised as mental health problems. For this reason, many people who struggle with hoarding have been pleased to see it included as a distinct and separate disorder. However, the definition of hoarding as a distinct disorder could potentially and wrongly imply a single cause (e.g. genes) or a single treatment (e.g. medication). While diagnosis may lead to access to mental health services, it will continue to be important that support and interventions are offered regardless of whether the person themselves identifies with the label of 'hoarder', particularly if functional impairment is high.

Difficulties with stigmatising and labelling people include the use of psychiatric descriptors such as 'insight' which are commonly found in the literature on hoarding. There is much research on the 'lack of insight' shown by people with hoarding difficulties; in one case, for instance, 21 per cent of a sample of people who hoard were described as lacking insight – significantly higher than those with OCD (Samuels et al., 2007).

> Lack of insight was more to do with total unawareness of the label ... it was total unawareness of that was what I was doing.
>
> Anon

A lack of insight has traditionally been ascribed to those service users who do not share the perspective of mental health professionals about their problems. Tolin et al. (2010) describe the common lack of awareness of the severity of difficulties among people who hoard, with over half described as having 'poor insight' or 'delusional'. However Tolin et al.'s work compared the discrepancy between how the individual viewed their problem and how relatives viewed it. They found a significant difference between both parties. One of the unique aspects of hoarding as a mental health problem is the obvious visible manifestation. For most mental health difficulties, significant others would not be asked to rate their perception of their relatives' problems.

When 'lack of insight' is used to describe the person who does not see themselves as a 'hoarder', the complexity of people's understanding of their own difficulties may be missed. A person without 'insight' may still acknowledge that they have a problem. Working psychologically to understand how they see the issue may be extremely valuable and enhance therapeutic engagement. Some people with hoarding difficulties refer to their problem as 'lack of storage', while others might say it is a 'not being able to get it straight' problem. Inappropriate labelling or use of judgemental, pejorative terms risks alienating people with hoarding difficulties and may lead to disengagement with services.

Much has been written about the damaging use of language and the importance of working with people on their own identified problems while recognising their resilience. Holding this balance between acknowledgement of a very real and disabling problem while keeping the person with difficulties central to our work without further stigmatising, is essential in understanding hoarding and offering appropriate services.

Now that hoarding problems have been recognised as a 'psychiatric diagnosis', clinicians who work with this client group have reflected on the impact. Mataix-Cols and Fernández de la Cruz (2018) consider it a 'Huge step in the right direction'. However, there are still many accounts of people being unable to access help from mental health services, and it remains an under-researched area.

Social and cultural influences

Hoarding needs to be considered in the wider context than as an individual difficulty. Problems arise in part due to social and material influences. The Midlands Psychology Group (2014) draw attention to the role of social inequality whether through class gender, ethnicity, sexuality or disability. Hoarding difficulties have been identified as more common amongst men, widows, the unemployed and those from less wealthy backgrounds (Samuels et al., 2008). Less is known about possible cultural differences.

> I believe there is a spiritual element in hoarding and letting go of possessions.
>
> Danielle

The environmental context in which the person lives will determine to some extent whether they identify as having a problem hoarding. The person who lives in a large detached home will be able to amass a much larger quantity of items before their home is very cluttered, in contrast to the person who rents a small flat and is living close to other people.

The social context for the individual is likely to have a significant part to play in (1) whether the hoard is considered problematic and (2) whether statutory services become involved. Many people are simply unaware that their rights to live as they might wish in their home are not straightforward in the eye of the law.

> I found that it wasn't worth forming emotional attachments, as most non-family that I grew attached to went away, for one reason or another, none were my fault but I didn't know that. This was just before my hoarding really took hold.
>
> Jim

Social isolation is a particularly key issue for people with hoarding difficulties. Both the person who hoards and their family members can become socially isolated (Wilbram et al., 2008). People with hoarding difficulties have been reported to distance themselves both from their families and from other forms of social support, possibly in order to neutralise others' attempts to manage the clutter (Sampson et al., 2012; Tompkins, 2011; Wilbram et al., 2008).

The effect of growing older and losing social support (through bereavement) is likely to interact with the increased difficulties faced by people as they grow older. Eckfield and Wallhagen (2013) describe two aspects of this: the loss of social buffering that a partner provides and the impact of inheritance of other's belongings on the person with hoarding difficulties. In addition, changing social roles as people retire will interact and may exacerbate hoarding, as identity, social connections and increased time available to acquire all impact on hoarding.

> *Nobody to hold me in check.*
> Martin

De la Cruz et al. (2016) makes the important point that the vast majority of studies into hoarding have been conducted in white westernised, industrialised societies. It is assumed that hoarding is a universal problem, but without transcultural studies this remains an assumption. There is a need for studies to establish the prevalence rates across cultures, the phenomenology of presentation across cultures and any differences in responses to psychological interventions. One study that has looked at hoarding from a transcultural perspective is Nordsletten et al. (2018). Through semi-structured interviews with participants in London, Barcelona, Fukuoka, and Rio de Janeiro, Nordsletten et al. (2018) found that the core beliefs and behaviours were consistent across these four groups. More studies with more cultural diversity are needed.

> *My experience, sadly, has been that help was just not available, so I long ago ceased bothering to ask for it, until now.*
> Harry

Why hoarding matters

It is important that people with hoarding difficulties get access to appropriate psychological interventions and advice that potentially can relieve distress or disability. Minimising or wrongly labelling hoarding can further alienate those who are in desperate situations, struggling, often in isolation, with little or no support. Recognition of the very real difficulties faced by people who hoard (and their friends, relatives and neighbours) might also mean that some of the issues affecting motivation to change and engagement with statutory services can be addressed. If the person with hoarding difficulties feels they are heard and respected without judgement, therapeutic efforts may pay dividends.

Hoarding links to significant levels of disability. A study by Nutley et al. (2022) using data from the Brain Health Registry found that hoarding severity was associated with areas of disability, including home management and self-care, mobility, and social and cognitive functioning. These impairments were equivalent to problems reported in chronic pain, major depressive disorder and diabetes. They suggest that interventions must go beyond home-related ones to target all the domains of functional impairment.

It is essential that those working with or supporting people with hoarding difficulties can also access services, training and advice. Identifying specific issues relevant to hoarding behaviour will increase our understanding and ability to offer appropriate interventions.

People can be both attached to and overwhelmed by their hoarding behaviour.

Prevalence rates of hoarding

Establishing prevalence of hoarding is not without its problems, as people who hoard have a tendency to minimise the problem (Tolin et al., 2010). Given also difficulties with shame and embarrassment, it would also seem likely that people with hoarding difficulties would disproportionately refuse to engage in research studies. Studies using a variety of case detection methods (Samuels et al., 2008; Iervolino et al., 2009; Mueller et al., 2009) have estimated hoarding behaviours as prevalent in 2–6 per cent of the population. Nordsletten et al.'s (2013a) well conducted, large prevalence study in the UK found a rate of 1.5 per cent. The most recent meta-analysis by Postlethwaite al. (2019) prevalence rates of 2.5 per cent with similar rates for men and women, though in the Nutley et al., (2023) study around 10 per cent of the large sample reported clinical or subclinical hoarding symptoms.

> *Bereavement just allowed it to go mad.*
> Martin

The development of hoarding difficulties tends to start around the age of 10 to 13 years. A study of children under the age of 10 years, by Frank et al. (2014), found the onset of hoarding with OCD was at a younger age than the onset of OCD without hoarding. Perhaps unsurprisingly, the expression of hoarding among children and young people shows some differences from that seen in adults. Plimpton et al. (2009) found that children had difficulties in discarding and maintaining control over possessions, but they did not have problems with clutter or excessive acquisition. This difference is partly associated with the controls put in place by parents, which prevent acquisitions overwhelming family living space. In addition to this, children simply have had less time to accumulate items than adults (Storch et al., 2011a).

Despite the early onset of hoarding difficulties, help seeking is less common before the age of 40 (Mackin et al., 2011). People with hoarding difficulties often come to the attention of services only in later life, as a result of specific later life issues such as downsizing property, or the bereavement of a significant other who had previously helped to mitigate the impact of hoarding behaviour (Eckfield & Wallhagen, 2013).

Severity and impact of hoarding is likely to increase over time. Indeed, in a survey of local health departments, Frost et al. (2000) observed that over 40 per cent of hoarding complaints involved agencies for older people. The impact of hoarding in later life can be exacerbated by physical illness, cognitive decline, limited mobility and health hazards (Ayers et al., 2011; Turner et al., 2010), and Eckfield and Wallhagen (2013) reported that hoarding disproportionally affects adults over 55 years of age.

Data on the prevalence of hoarding by people with ID is limited. However, it is estimated that about 16 per cent of children with ID engage in hoarding that is not linked to either OCD and/or autism (Testa et al., 2011). Sixty per cent of people with PWS have been shown to hoard (Storch et al., 2011a).

Hoarding is particularly common in people with ASC, both with and without ID, 33 per cent of whom are estimated to collect material that is related to their special interest (South et al., 2005).

How hoarding can affect people's lives

Part 2: How hoarding can affect people's lives

Key points

Hoarding can put people at risk in many ways.

Difficulties associated with hoarding can be physical and social as well as psychological.

The effects of hoarding extend to family, friends and neighbours, and more widely to interactions with other community services.

Physical health

The health needs of those with severe and complex mental health problems have long been known to be worse than in the general population. People with severe hoarding difficulties are likely to be at risk of neglecting their own physical healthcare needs and have greater difficulty accessing physical health services. Increasing isolation increases the likelihood that the person may not be known to local GPs, thus creating further risk that physical health is compromised.

People with hoarding difficulties have been shown to be nearly three times more likely to be overweight or obese, and significantly more likely to report a wide range of chronic and severe medical problems (Tolin et al., 2008a), with the most common conditions including diabetes, seizures, head injury, sleep apnoea, and cardiovascular, arthritic, haematological and lung conditions (Ayers et al., 2014). The directionality and reasons for this relationship are unknown, but it is clear that many of these conditions would interfere with people's ability to manage a cluttered home environment and demonstrates the importance of assessing physical health and capability. The risks for older adults are that existing medical conditions may be exacerbated due to unsanitary housing and reduced access to health professionals (Novack, 2010).

In addition, if someone is taken seriously ill and calls for an ambulance, difficulties can arise with access. If access for the ambulance service (or fire service who may assist in certain circumstances), is compromised, there is little hope that the person lying ill could be rescued and taken to hospital. This leaves the person and potentially their family particularly vulnerable in cases of emergency.

The presence of significant numbers of rats or other pests can lead to animal urine and faeces being trapped within or under possessions. As this decays over time, ammonia will be released into the air affecting the air quality and potentially causing breathing difficulties (Reinisch, 2008).

The need for people working in this area to think about physical health has been highlighted by the study of Nutley et al. (2021), who found that those diagnosed with hoarding disorder had significantly higher rates of medical comorbidity

than those without. In addition, people with subclinical levels of hoarding, that is, they did not meet the diagnostic criteria but showed some hoarding features, also had raised levels of medical conditions. Therefore, if the person is agreeable when working with a person with hoarding problems, a thorough assessment of physical health problems and direction to appropriate care is advisable.

Self-neglect

If the person is unable to access hot water or a bathroom or simply the sink, self-care becomes increasingly unlikely and difficult. The person may find it difficult to wash clothes or keep themselves clean. This can exacerbate difficulties with isolation if the person increasingly avoids contact with other people.

> *It blocks up your house. You can't use it for what it's meant to be used for.*
> Danielle

Alternatively, they may engage in more acquisition behaviours, buying new clothes in the absence of any readily available clean clothes in the home. Difficulties accessing the kitchen may lead to problems with eating and drinking. This can range from people who are unable to heat any food up, or keep anything used for eating clean, or store food in unusual places where it may rapidly deteriorate, be forgotten or be eaten when well past its best.

Difficulties with organisational abilities regarding bill-paying can lead to services being removed, increasing risk that the home cannot be heated or that the phone is disconnected. The person may be aware of faults in the heating or water system, that lead to them turning off their own water supply in an attempt to prevent further problems. If this becomes a long-standing solution, the person can end up living without essential services and support. Self-neglect issues now need to be considered in relation to the Care Act 2014.

SQUALOR, HOARDING AND SELF-NEGLECT

Previously, a person living in a consistently and significantly unclean and disorganised home would be referred to as suffering from Diogenes Syndrome (DS; Proctor & Rahman, 2022). This is now an outdated term and the terminology better used is that the person is residing in Severe Domestic Squalor (SDS). Thus, the hoarding disorder (HD) is the presenting clinical condition, whereas the SDS is the grossly unsanitary living environment in the home. SDS has been defined as when '…a person's home is so unclean, messy and unhygienic that people of similar culture and background would consider extensive clearing and cleaning to be essential' (Snowdon, Halliday & Banerjee, 2012). There is also the condition of severe self-neglect (SNS) and this refers to global aspects of personal neglect and not just the environmental neglect that is apparent in HD and SDS. Therefore, in SNS there is (a) an absence of self-care to the degree that creates personal ill health, (b) neglect of personal hygiene routines, (c) a passive inability to avoid harm as a result of self-neglect, (d) a lack of help seeking and (e) an unwillingness to manage one's personal affairs. When asked to assess and intervene in HD, it is also therefore important to consider and assess SDS and SNS. For example, in SNS, the person maybe living in a non-hoarded house, but neglecting their personal hygiene, their diet, and/or ignoring the management of ongoing medical interventions.

OVERLAPS AND DIFFERENCES

This is a complex area because of the environmental similarities between houses that are hoarded and those that are more defined by the presence of squalor. Both HD and SDS are a challenge to assess in situ, as both environments can result in physiological reactions of disgust, and this is likely to be enhanced where the home is squalid. Both HD and SDS are clinically complex conditions with diverse contributory underlying aetiologies and risk factors and varying current contingencies of reinforcement. Across both HD and SDS there is the clear accumulation of possessions and rubbish beyond the norm for a typical matched home. This similarity of outward appearance of hoarded and squalid homes therefore risks neglect of the identification of the differences between the conditions and the associated person-centred formulation. A hoarded home can be without signs of squalor, but a squalid home would typically also be hoarded and where the two conditions overlap, the home is both hoarded and squalid. In HD, the accumulation of objects and possessions is more active (and often the result of compulsive acquisition patterns and enhanced emotional attachments) and in SDS, the accumulation is more passive and less emotionally primed. The evidence base for SDS has not developed at the same rate as HD and SN. However, a recent panel study meta-analysis conducted on the English Household Survey generated an estimated squalor prevalence of 0.85 per cent (Norton et al., 2024). This slower development of an evidence base is presumably due to the absence of valid and reliable clinical assessment tools.

IMPACTS

When HD and SDS co-exist then about one quarter of those people will have a physical health problem that creates risks of reducing the necessary discard rates such as being incontinent, having mobility issues or having severe visual impairments (Snowdon, Shah & Halliday, 2007). The safety risks of both hoarded and squalid homes are similar in terms of risk of crush injury, trip and fall injuries, being physically trapped and the heightened fire load (Frost, Steketee & Williams, 2000). In terms of squalor, the state of the home adds also to the environmental threat with risk of insect and rodent infestation and lack of general hygiene increasing the chance of personal infection, and then repeated infection as the infection might get treated, but the environmental trigger remains the same. SDS like HD often creates problems with neighbours who have understandable concerns relating to fear of infestation and the risks associated with heightened fire loads. Removing possessions through clearances for SDS can be stressful, if mass clearances are used, valuable and irreplaceable possessions may be lost. Care needs to be taken in limiting the psychological effects.

Social isolation and loneliness

Social isolation and loneliness are associated with hoarding problems. A hoarded home becomes a source of embarrassment and even shame for people, making it a place they cannot invite people to. Davidson et al. (2020), in a study of people with a diagnosis of hoarding disorder who were seeking help, found that 48 per cent lived alone, 48 per cent said family and friends never visited, 33 per cent allowed no one into their home, 55 per cent did report phoning a family member or friend at least nine times a month.

Edwards' et al. (2023) found that people with a diagnosis of hoarding disorder experienced increased levels of thwarted belongingness and loneliness when compared to both a control group and a group with OCD. Similarly, Yap (2023) found that when people from a help-seeking group diagnosed with hoarding disorder were compared to a matched group from the general population, the group of people with hoarding problems had significantly higher levels of loneliness. Yap suggests that this means loneliness needs to be assessed and addressed as part of the care offered to people with hoarding problems. Perhaps this is one of the needs partly met by hoarding support groups.

Families

Buscher et al. (2013) summarise the effects of hoarding on families under three themes:

- quality of life
- shattered families
- rallying around.

The theme 'quality of life' describes the wellbeing of relatives, whereas 'shattered families' includes the impact of hoarding on family relationships and the loss of 'normal' family lives.

The theme 'rallying around' describes various responses that families have to the hoarding, both positive and negative.

For example, families are typically eager to help, but can get drawn into colluding with the hoarding as a response strategy.

> *I as a carer am left with my own feelings also with no one to talk to. It is isolating and lonely.*
>
> Julie

Families of those who compulsively hoard may experience embarrassment, shame and worry linked to the hoarding, and may struggle with compulsive hoarding behaviours or urges of their own (Sampson, 2013). It may be that only one member of the family actually wants change, and will have to work with other relatives continuing to acquire items, while they are trying to reduce this behaviour.

Relatives make comparisons between the past and the present environmental situation, as well as detailing the current level of clutter in the house, in order to illustrate the impact hoarding has on 'normalcy' (Wilbram et al., 2008). They can feel a sense of loss as 'normal' family life and family norms and values, such as eating together at a table, inviting friends to visit or decorating the house for Christmas, are eroded. These are just some of the family rituals and traditions which may be lost in households where someone has hoarding difficulties. Adult children of hoarders have expressed this as the loss of the safe environment that once was their childhood home (Sampson, 2013).

Research by Rees et al. (2020) with adults whose parents were hoarders when they were children had three key findings: the social isolation created for the children as they were more reluctant to make friends, the psychological strengths they developed from living with a parent with hoarding problems, and the need for more support and information for children in this position.

The care of children and young people in the home of someone who hoards can be severely compromised. It may cause them embarrassment and they may be unwilling to bring friends home. It may be difficult for them to do homework, or keep their school work organised due to limited surfaces or table space available. In more extreme cases, it may prove difficult for them to sleep in their own bed or bedroom. Their clothes may be kept in a separate area of the house. There may be no floor space in which to play with toys. It may become so difficult for the parent to function that the child is not able to eat ordinary food, and may not be able to wash or have clean clothes. In more extreme situations, children may need to be cared for away from their home and parent(s). The number of people with hoarding difficulties who have had a child removed due to their difficulty in resolving the impact on their living environment is estimated to be up to three per cent (Tolin et al., 2008a).

Drury et al. (2014) found a significantly greater carer burden for relatives of people who hoard compared with relatives of collectors. Family members of people with hoarding problems also report higher levels of rejecting attitudes toward their relative, than seen in families where one person has OCD (Tolin et al., 2008b). The level of squalor reported by relatives was a significant predictor of carer burden and functional impairment for family members. Similarly, the rejecting attitudes reported by relatives were found to be predicted by the severity of the hoarding (Tolin et al., 2008b).

Family relationships can be put under strain by hoarding behaviour.

Co-habiting with a person who hoards was found to be a significant predictor of carer burden and functional impairment (Drury et al., 2014). Nordsletten et al. (2014) found that blood relatives (e.g. parents, children) of people who hoard reported higher burden scores than spouses. Despite this, spouses have reported higher distress scores than children of compulsive hoarders (Frost et al., 2011b).

> *My wife would say: 'I'm going to throw it all out.' No! No! No! I need it.*
> Anon

Housing

Hoarding behaviour that compromises the ability of gas/electric services to be inspected or maintained leads to higher risk of faults developing, house fires starting and/or dangerous gas leaks.

> *I want this room back, and I want a room upstairs.*
> Danielle

Many housing associations require reasonable access to property and may not be able to enter the home of someone who hoards; if utility services are not able to be maintained, the risk increases that landlords will evict tenants. Tolin et al. (2008a) found that 8–12 per cent of people who hoard have been threatened with or experienced eviction.

Losing post in the morass of objects can increase the risk of eviction, because the person may not necessarily be aware that the process has been initiated. Housing providers face the difficult task of working with people who may be unknown to mental health care services, and may receive little or no specialist psychological consultation or supervision in their work.

Hoarding is located in the home and
can be a hidden problem.

There are many people with ID and/or ASC or complex, severe mental health difficulties, or older adults who live in supported tenancies, residential homes or nursing homes. This can lead to additional difficulties, as hoarding may well affect the lives of both co-residents and staff working in the homes. Disagreements between staff groups involved in providing care can arise, with staff from one service experiencing pressure from staff in other services to clear the room of belongings, despite the person themselves showing no wish or interest in doing this work. The clash in values from different providers of services can exacerbate general tensions. Some providers may be more willing to 'do to' clients, whereas others may see their role as supporting the client to exercise choice or take personal responsibility.

Accidents and fire

Hoarding leaves a person (and their relatives) at high risk of accidents. Piles of belongings can become unstable and slide or fall. This can lead to people being trapped or seriously injured. Piles of objects can put strain on the physical structure of the property with disastrous results. Ceilings can collapse as a result of the weight of stored possessions, doorways can be damaged and walls weakened.

The risks of this are borne out by Australian research data which showed that although less than 0.25 per cent of house fires were of people with hoarding difficulties, 24 per cent of fire-related deaths were of people who hoard (Steketee & Frost, 2014a). The risks for older adults are even greater. As mobility and balance decreases, what once may have been manageable living conditions can become increasingly dangerous (Novack, 2010).

Recent figures from the London Fire Brigade from 2023 indicate that in the previous year, they attended nearly 1,040 hoarding-related fires, including 186 injuries and 10 deaths (LFB, 2023). Because of their involvement with hoarding-related fire incidents, the fire service around the UK had taken a leading position in wanting to address this problem. Fire services often offer a range of support for people with hoarding problems, including fitting smoke alarms, developing harm minimisation strategies, hosting support groups, inputting to multi-agency frameworks, and providing good, psychologically informed information online.

Financial costs

If people are living with a huge amount of possessions, they may not be able to access their financial paperwork. They may not be working, but also may not be claiming benefits to which they are entitled. This increases the risk of them living in poverty and becoming more marginalised from society.

Maintaining attendance at work appears to be more challenging for people with hoarding difficulties than for those with other mental health problems, with Tolin et al.'s research (2008a) suggesting that people who hoard had an average of seven work-impairment days in a month. This places them at higher risk of losing their jobs, and thus potentially increasing their financial difficulties and isolation. In addition, losing a job may have significant impact on their sense of identity.

The costs incurred by outside agencies attempting to help or resolve the problem can quickly escalate. Mental health services may pay to have homes cleared, but may find the person becomes highly distressed at the manner in which the clearing was done and is unable to maintain change.

Environmental health departments are typically managing about four cases of hoarding per year. Of these, between one and two has no mental health services involvement (Holroyd & Price, 2009). Environmental health officers are often left trying to negotiate clearance, then using legal means to permit forced clearance. All of this entails significant cost, and while environmental health services may attempt to recoup their costs, this is often not possible and may require further lengthy legal work and additional expense.

So, problems with hoarding have a financial cost for the individual with hoarding and the wider society. These costs are starting to be researched. Neave et al. (2017), in a scoping study of the economic costs of hoarding disorder in the Northeast, found that whilst people with hoarding: 'comprise a relatively small sample of the population, they constitute a significant economic burden to housing providers and emergency services. In addition to the direct economic costs there are additional economic costs in relation to disability and unemployment benefits, and costs to the social and health services.' (Neave et al., p.5). These costs need more research to incentivise initiatives to help people with the problem that reducing the prevalence of hoarding will positively impact public finances overall.

Assessment of
hoarding difficulties

Part 3: Assessment of hoarding difficulties

Key points

Formulation requires psychosocial assessment as well as a physical assessment of the living environment.

Assessment and action should be preceded by an agreement between the clinical psychologist and the client on the way they will work together.

Addressing motivation difficulties must be central to improve engagement. Assessment tools and interview schedules can facilitate assessment.

There are considerable benefits in involving others, such as carers and other services, in assessment, formulation and intervention.

Cognisance of relevant legislation is required, although statutory powers should be used with caution.

In working with people referred for help with hoarding, as with any mental health problem, prior to formulation a period of psychological assessment is required. The difference with hoarding is that the assessment also requires an environmental assessment of the home and other buildings (e.g. sheds), in combination with personal history and current thoughts, feelings, behaviours and interpersonal relationships.

> *Others mean well but just cannot understand your difficulties. 'Just pull yourself together,' 'Keep smiling' as a friend says to me... I am trying hard but need a hand up, not lecturing.*
>
> Harry

Assessment

PHILOSOPHY OF CARE

In order to best provide therapy, care and/or on-going management, it is important to remain non-judgemental while holding on to hope that things can change. The person themselves may have been subject to repeated draconian-style treatment and/or pressure from others. Forcible house clearance may have left a person quite traumatised and unwilling to work collaboratively for understandable reasons. They may themselves think they need to sort their life out, but despite repeated attempts have not made much progress.

> *What helped was admitting I had a problem.*
>
> Martin

This context makes the role of those in therapeutic positions even more significant if they are able to stand alongside the person they are working with or consider whether or not it is the right time for treatment. Respect for the person is paramount. The inclusion of a co-worker who can join the practitioner psychologist to work with family members and offer family intervention meetings, may be an essential step. Involving support staff or assistant psychologists can also be beneficial in setting and offering exposure-type work.

Progress is typically slow and therapeutic contracts need to reflect this and be based on measurable and clearly stated goals. Holding on to respect for the person and staying non-judgemental is particularly challenging when the pace of change feels glacial and the impact of the amount of possessions is causing harm to others.

It can be extremely pressurised working alongside people who are surrounded by a large number of others insisting on change. The tendency to get drawn into expert-like directing or advising can be strong, but it is essential to try to remain collaborative and focused on the wishes of the individual who has difficulties with hoarding. Tolin et al. (2012) describe the impact on the work of professional attitudes. Health-care workers surveyed described working with people who hoard as frustrating, quite a negative experience, and having a poorer working alliance with the client. This draws attention to the need to remain diligent and interpersonally flexible and responsive when building and maintaining a good working relationship, modifying treatment when indicated, repairing ruptures to the alliance and paying particular attention to our own thoughts of hopelessness.

Practitioner psychologists need to consider engagement issues carefully with people who hoard, due to variations in shared understanding of the difficulties, the high degree of shame people who hoard may feel about the appearance of their home, and the likely high level of criticism they may have received from others over many years.

Difficulties with assessment are multiplied when the person themselves hasn't requested help. Access to appropriate services must be considered. The impact on others must be a part of assessment and be taken into consideration once decisions about appropriate services are being made. Addressing motivation will be a key part of assessment. As with any mental health issue, finding out what is causing distress, rather than pre-judging is essential. Identifying the thoughts that interfere with recognising that there is a problem and identifying subsequent behaviour change is important.

If people disengage from traditional services, it may reflect a perceived lack of usefulness of those services (BPS, 2013b). People with hoarding difficulties often present in services as a result of other people or agencies (such as housing providers) identifying a problem, rather than the person themselves. Being subject to threats of eviction or being compulsorily detained often worsen any attempts at engagement. Psychological intervention can easily appear to work to the same agenda as legal forces. Engaging in identifying and working to the priorities of the client may in fact lead to not addressing hoarding concerns at all. However, generic recovery-focused work can be a valuable way of gaining credibility of having something useful to offer. This can then potentially open the door into options for psychological intervention. The tension for practitioner psychologists is then between keeping in mind the client's goals and the needs of relatives and the wider community.

> *I wanted to get support without being judged or stigmatised.*
>
> Anon

Assessment of older people requires an understanding of the customs and 'cohort beliefs' of those born in earlier generations (e.g. Knight, 1999; Laidlaw et al., 2003). This is an important consideration both in terms of beliefs about psychiatric or psychological input, and also with regard to

> *I will be able to fix that.*
>
> Harry

beliefs about hoarding itself. For example, a history of deprivation or rationing could lead to the development of core beliefs about the importance of saving and avoiding waste that increase vulnerability to hoarding.

Clear, documented agreements and actions need to be put in place at every step of the engagement process with the client. This will foster an atmosphere of collaborative working, rather than the impression of applying therapies unilaterally. While this working contract can be verbally agreed with the person prior to starting any work, it can usefully be written down, and typically should contain agreement on:

- what areas of the house the practitioner psychologist is able to work in, with the client;
- whether the practitioner psychologist needs to seek approval before touching items;
- what to do with valuables that are unearthed during de-cluttering;
- safety issues in the face of precariously stored hoards; and
- what should happen to any items that it is mutually agreed will be discarded.

In order to assess the person's situation and needs effectively, a blend of out-patient and home visits should be considered. Out-patient appointments may be necessary to complete clinical assessments (without the distraction or uncomfortableness of the home environment) and domiciliary visits are vital to assess the level at which the rooms in the home function. Without visiting the home environment, it can

> *I let very few people into my home; it is always an issue if I let people visit.*
> Anon

be difficult to get an accurate assessment of the extent of the problem. If the person is reluctant for workers to visit their home then issues of shame should be addressed, rather than minimised.

Measures

MEASURES: IDIOGRAPHIC AND NOMOTHETIC

The use of measures when working with people that hoard is useful both in terms of the assessment of the presenting problem, the presence of comorbidity, in the evaluation of outcomes on the short-term and also indexing the durability (or not) of the psychological intervention provided. Because the relapse rate has yet to be reliably estimated, then the use of measures over follow-up time is indicated. It is best to complete measures directly with the person and it is useful to collect measures during the conduct of domiciliary visits and this be integrated into that activity. Speaking to third parties is useful in terms of cross-referencing the information gained from formal measures and interviews. Should the person decline to be interviewed, then accessing a reliant informant can be useful here. The assessment of insight also benefits from taking into consideration the views and opinions of other reliable informants.

CHOICE OF MEASURES AND EVALUATING CHANGE

In this context, it is advisable to use both idiographic measures (i.e. measures that have personal relevance to the service user and can also be used to assess progress towards personal treatment goals) and also nomothetic measures (i.e. measures that have undergone a psychometric evaluation process and therefore there are norms and also progress can be considered in terms of reliable and clinically significant change; RCSC). For those people with difficulties with self-reporting, assessment may need to rely on clinician assessment and this be complimented with third-party assessments and also the assessment of behavioural products (see idiographic measures section below). All nomothetic and idiographic measures need to be integrated into a full psychological assessment – taken alone the measures should not be used to signify caseness or not. Measurement also contributes to the construction of case formulations.

IDIOGRAPHIC MEASURES

An idiographic assessment of what is being hoarded is often required, which can involve counting the amount of, for example, shoes, flyers, food, pens or bodily waste that a person has accumulated and then stored. In terms of the number of objects coming into the home, a daily idiographic count of the number of items that were acquired and/or bought that day could also be useful. The reduction in such counts would be a powerful analysis of change to share with the service user. The graphing of such outcomes over time is indicated and formal evaluation can take place in terms of the use of non-overlap statistics. Because of the tendency to shift objects around the home, without actually discarding them (i.e. 'churning'), then it is important that idiographic measures take into account this tendency, so that any idiographic measurement is indeed accurate. There is no formal nomothetic measure of churning. Because people that hoard have often been hoarding since adolescence (Zaboski et al., 2019), then it is important the idiographic measures and goals also reflect an achievable target for the person.

NOMOTHETIC MEASURES

A number of useful measures have been developed and evaluated as the hoarding evidence has evolved. It is important here to separate measures of the mechanisms of hoarding (such as object attachment) or the outcome (i.e. the reduction in levels of clutter in the home). Mechanisms are the targets for intervention that create changes in the outcomes and so utilising measures of both mechanism and outcome are therefore useful. Similarly, it is useful to blend the selection of clinician-administered and also self-report measures of mechanisms and outcome. The selection of appropriate junctures for the administration of such measures needs to fit with the psychological approach being used. The minimum would be pre- and post-psychological intervention, but completing measures post-formulation, and at the end of treatment phases (e.g. shifting from behavioural to cognitive approaches) can also be usefully considered. Again, the importance of the use of measurement during structured follow-up comes to the fore here.

Reliable change is where the change observed on the outcome measure is beyond doubt and clinically significant change is where the service user's scores move into the community population. Jacobson and Truax (1991) explain how to operationalise reliable clinically significant change. The use of RCSC is helpful in terms of assessing relapse over the follow-up period. In terms of measures, then the structured followed up of people that hoard is a valuable opportunity to track outcomes using RCSC concepts. This is also a valuable opportunity to share with the service user signs of progress, statis and relapse and should trigger associated remedial actions. See the section on the Savings Inventory Revised for an example.

THE CLUTTER IMAGE RATING SCALE

The Clutter Image Rating Scale (CIRS; Frost et al., 2008) is a clinician completed outcome measure and this measures the degree of clutter in the rooms (i.e. kitchen, living room and bedroom) of the home. The CIRS has been psychometrically validated and is simple to use – unless levels of clutter are so high in the home that it is difficult physically to stand back from all the possessions. If there are mobility issues that prevent a person from accessing all the room in the home, then the CIRS can be rated on photographic evidence (and this can be the case for when the person attends in clinic). The CIRS uses a 9-point visual scale, a score of 4 or more indexes clutter in that room that is sufficient to warrant intervention. In terms of assessing and having a shared understanding of the problem, it is also useful to co-rate rooms using the CIRS with a person who hoards to 'see if they see what you see'. This can therefore be used as a proxy measure of insight. Differences are fruitful avenues for exploration. This 'compare and contrast' with the CIRS can be done in terms of the evaluation of outcome also and to see whether perceptions have aligned over the course of the intervention (i.e. 'are we seeing the same thing now?'). This would also therefore show a proxy improvement in insight. The CIRS can also be used to have a room to target for intervention and then demonstrate change as the other rooms can serve as the 'control' and can then be targeted over time. The graphing and sharing of this progress would be a valuable source of evidence for improvement and when a room crosses into the community range (i.e. <4 and therefore a clinical change), then this can be highlighted on case tracking graphs. Again, change compared against a control room in the house can be helpful here.

STRUCTURED INTERVIEW FOR HOARDING DISORDER

The Structured Interview for Hoarding Disorder (SIHD; Nordsletten et al., 2013b) is clinician completed interview. The closed questions contained in the interview schedule relate to each of the six DSM-5 diagnostic criteria for Hoarding Disorder and also has two specifiers concerning levels of insight (i.e. from good/fair, to poor insight, to an absence of insight) and excessive acquisition (yes/no). The SIHD is useful in the effort to distinguish hoarding from non-pathological collecting, as well as other disorders that might have a significant collecting component, such as OCD or brain injury. The SIHD contains a risk section that is unscored but is a useful tool.

SAVING INVENTORY REVISED

The Saving Inventory-Revised (SI-R; Frost et al., 2004) is a self-report measure of the severity of hoarding problems. It has received the most psychometric evaluation work and has therefore often been used as an outcome measure in the treatment evidence base. The SI-R contains 23 items that are scored from 0–4 and comprises three subscales of (1) difficulty with discarding, (2) clutter and (3) excessive acquisition. Service users that score >40 are considered a case on the SI-R. In terms of the RCSC on the SI-R, when the SI-R reduces by 20 and the final score is <38, then this case can be considered recovered. Those for whom the SI-R score reduces by >20 but they remain >38 on the SI-R total then this case can be considered improved, but not recovered. If the intervention creates an increase >20 on the SI-R, then this case can be considered a case of deterioration. Where the SI-R change does not exceed 20 points, then this can be labelled as not changed (Norberg, Chasson & Tolin, 2021). Change rates on the SI-R are valuable sources of input for the effective clinical supervision of cases.

COMPULSIVE ACQUISITION SCALE

The Compulsive Acquisition Scale (CAS; Frost et al., 2002) is a self-report measure that contains 18-items, and these are all scored from 1 (not at all) to 7 (very much or often). The CAS measures the extent and severity to which a person feels the need to acquire possessions. This is therefore a measure of the 'possession input' into the home. It may be the case that reducing input into the home may be an early (and possibly more achievable behavioural goal) and changes to this can be indexed with the CAS. The CAS has two subscales the CAS-Buy (an index of compulsive buying behaviours measured over 12 items) and CAS-Free (an index of compulsive acquisition measured over 6 items).

OTHER MEASURES

There are no specific hoarding assessments for people with cognitive impairments, but formal measures such as the Child Saving Inventory (Storch et al., 2011b) may be useful. In the specific case of hoarding associated with PWS, Clarke et al. (2002) developed the Prader-Willi Structured Interview Questionnaire that examines both ritualistic and OCD-type behaviours, which may have clinical utility in developing case formulations with people with PWS.

A hoarding assessment interview

This assessment interview is in two parts:

The first part is for the initial assessment to ascertain motivation for change

The second part is for assessing the hoarding behaviour in greater detail should the person want to work on their hoarding.

Making a change to a person's living environment can be a profound thing to do. The clinician needs to remember this at all times, particularly during the initial assessment. It is easy to jump to conclusions that because it is so obvious to you, you and the client agree on what exactly the problem is that they are prepared to collaboratively work on. In the first assessment session, bear in mind the cycle of change and where the client may be on it. Do not assume that they want change. If the client does want change, agree collaboratively on what they want to be different, then there is a follow-up interview which can be used if the person is asking for help with hoarding and is focused on addressing the hoarding. If the person identifies other difficulties, and you are able to support them with these, this can allow trust to develop and potentially reviewing goals for intervention collaboratively. The order of questions may need to change in response to the answers to previous questions.

PART ONE: QUESTIONS FOR INITIAL ASSESSMENT AND MOTIVATION FOR CHANGE

1. What do you see as the main problem at the moment? Can you tell me more about that?

2. What is causing you distress or frustration at the moment?

3. What led to you coming to meet with me?

4. Is anything about your living situation, your home, causing you problems or distress?

5. Have other people said to you that your living environment needs to change? What do you think about what they say?

6. What would you like to do that is difficult at the moment? Are there things you can't do because of the difficulties??

7. Is there anything about your living environment that you would like to be different?

8. What have you tried in order to sort this difficulty out? (the difficulty might not be described as a hoarding problem. But could be described as 'unable to have visitors' or 'my neighbours constantly complaining' or other related problems)

9. What did you learn from trying that?

10. What else have you thought about trying to do?

11. Do you consider your living environment to be how you would want it to be?

12. Do you consider that you need more storage? What have you done about this? What do others say about your need for storage?

Do you think that you have any difficulties with any or all of the following:

    i. Buying things that you do not need? Tell me more about that…

    ii. Organising the things that you have? In what way?

    iii. Keeping your things clean? In what way? Do other people comment about this?

13. Getting rid of things? Often people have understandable and real concerns about throwing things away, can you tell me about what goes through your mind if we were to throw something away?

    i. Do you consider that throwing things away is wasteful?

    ii. Do you think that throwing things away would be harmful to the environment?

    iii. Do you keep things because they might come in useful one day?

PART TWO: QUESTIONS FOR ASSESSING HOARDING BEHAVIOURS

If the client states that hoarding is a problem and they want help to address their hoarding behaviour, the following questions can be asked either at the same session or at the next. Sometimes it might be productive to let them have time to reflect and to ask these questions at a second session. Sometimes it will be best to seize the day and ask them at the first appointment. Clinical judgement will determine which approach to follow. Use the CIRS as part of the assessment.

1. Please can we have a look at each room in your house and tell me what you do and do not like about them and what you would like to change?

2. Can you tell me what things are most important to you in your home? For example, if you were told that you had 30 minutes to evacuate the property, what would you take with you?

3. What are the objects and items in your house that would be easiest for you to get rid of?

4. Tell me about how you acquire things: what do you buy, where and when? What are you given?

5. How do you organise your things: do you have strategies and plans for how you do this? If not, would you like to develop some?

6. What is your current routine for cleaning your home? Would you like to change it at all?

7. How do you get rid of things from your home? Do you:

    i. Bin things that you do not need at regular intervals?

    ii. Put things in the charity bin or give things to charity shops?

    iii. Give things to friends?

    iv. Take things to car boot sales?

8. What areas of the house would you like help with working on?

9. Do I have permission to touch things?

10. What will we do if we find valuables whilst sorting?

11. What shall we agree about the safety of working in some rooms if they are very cluttered – what is our agreement to keep safe?

12. What is our agreement about discarding items and what happens to them when they are gone?

Developed by Whomsley and Holmes

Involving others: Carers and other services

Working with people affected by hoarding behaviour can be just as effective as working with the individual themselves. A focus which is solely individualistic will miss the complexity of the difficulties associated with hoarding.

> *I want to get it sorted so I don't leave my children with the muddle.*
> Danielle

A first step may be to identify who is involved. For example, housing support workers may not be aware of the involvement of mental health services. Until recently, it was not unheard of for a person to have several different agencies supporting them, all of which are unaware of each other. The problem of many agencies being involved and not being aware of one another has been attempted to be addressed over the last ten years with the development of multi-agency hoarding frameworks that are freely available on the internet. These give a set of guidance, a protocol and resources. County councils and Safeguarding boards usually host them.

The motivation to change of the person who hoards may be enhanced by involving others affected by the hoarding behaviour. It would seem essential to identify the effects on others as part of a thorough assessment, even if the person themselves views things differently. The views of those sharing the home or visiting can be helpful in addressing reasons to make changes.

> *I've had pressure from others, my friends and family would be on at me... why do you do it? ...the state of the house...*
> Anon

The assessment can be informed by clarifying the goals of those affected in behavioural terms. Being specific and focused can increase the chance that change can happen. Facilitating discussions between all concerned can help move vague comments, such as 'it needs to be cleared', to more focused comments based on practical considerations, such as 'the plumber needs access to the radiators' or 'the bin bags in the front garden need to be moved'.

When working with networks, Practitioner psychologists can mistakenly assume everyone holds the same values and thinks alike. In practice, organisations differ; even teams within the same service can hold conflicting views on the ability of people to clear their homes. Carers and external agencies can benefit from support in identifying priorities and areas that are essential to clear versus things that can be left, or worked on in the future. Practitioner psychologists may be able to facilitate the clarification of expectations and understanding, and set clear, achievable behavioural goals for change.

In summary, therefore, the assessment of hoarding requires an integrated environmental assessment and also a traditional biopsychosocial assessment in order to attain an holistic picture of the person's difficulties; Practitioner psychologists need to accept that assessment may take some time.

Formulation

The most researched model of hoarding comes from a cognitive-behavioural understanding of distress. A cognitive behavioural (CB) model of hoarding developed by Steketee and Frost (2014a) is reproduced in Figure 1.

Figure 1: A cognitive behavioural model of hoarding (Steketee & Frost (2014a, 2007), reproduced with the permission of Oxford University Press, USA).

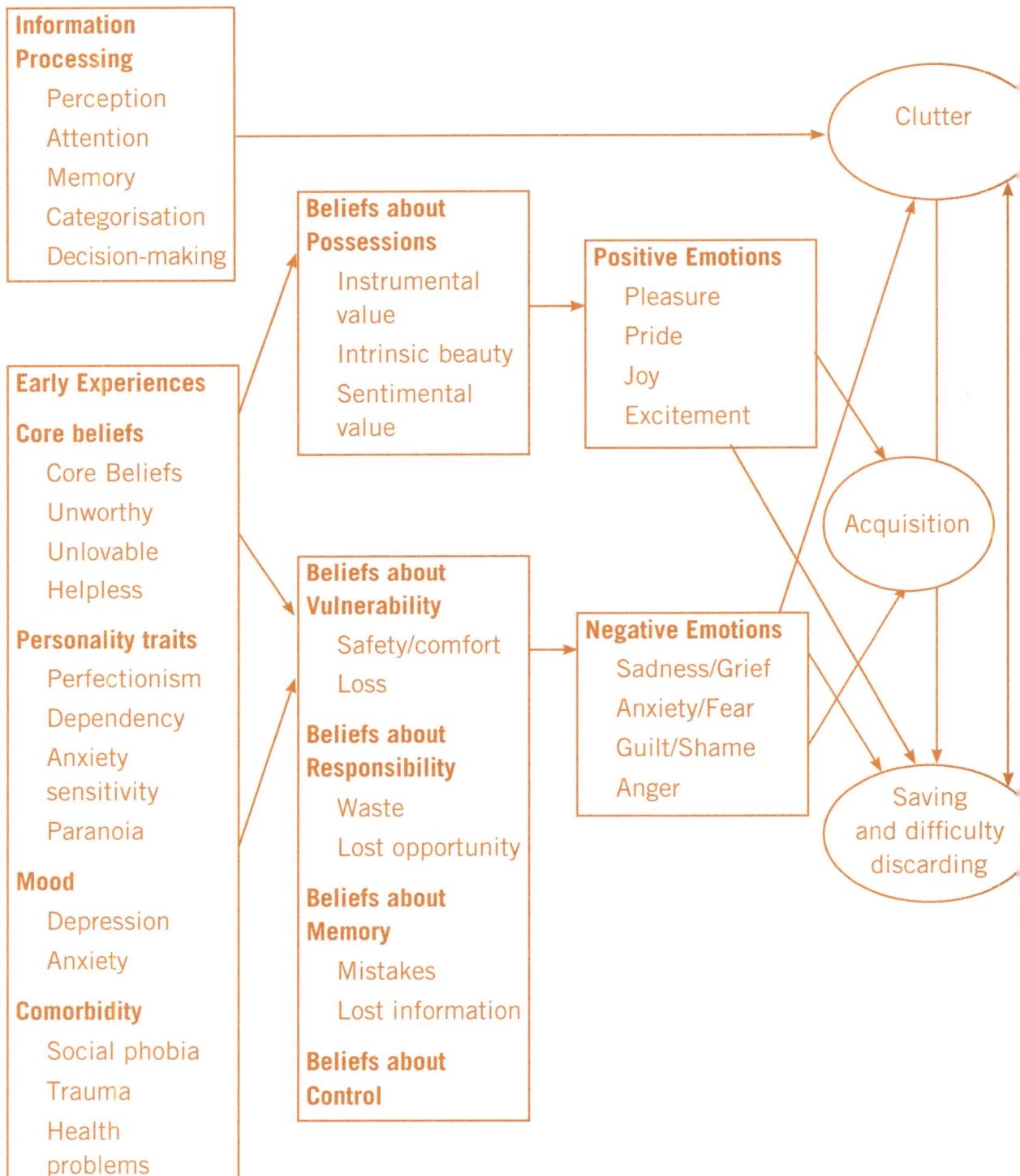

Information Processing
- Perception
- Attention
- Memory
- Categorisation
- Decision-making

Early Experiences

Core beliefs
- Core Beliefs
- Unworthy
- Unlovable
- Helpless

Personality traits
- Perfectionism
- Dependency
- Anxiety sensitivity
- Paranoia

Mood
- Depression
- Anxiety

Comorbidity
- Social phobia
- Trauma
- Health problems

Beliefs about Possessions
- Instrumental value
- Intrinsic beauty
- Sentimental value

Beliefs about Vulnerability
- Safety/comfort
- Loss

Beliefs about Responsibility
- Waste
- Lost opportunity

Beliefs about Memory
- Mistakes
- Lost information

Beliefs about Control

Positive Emotions
- Pleasure
- Pride
- Joy
- Excitement

Negative Emotions
- Sadness/Grief
- Anxiety/Fear
- Guilt/Shame
- Anger

Clutter

Acquisition

Saving and difficulty discarding

Predisposing factors might include information-processing difficulties and personality traits (e.g. perfectionism or anxiety sensitivity), and early experiences which may increase a likelihood of problems developing include the development of core beliefs such as 'I'm unworthy' or 'I'm unlovable'.

Positive beliefs about the value of possessions will lead to positive emotions such as pride/excitement, whereas negative beliefs about responsibility or memory can lead to negative emotions such as sadness, anger or fear. These are perpetuated by behaviours such as acquiring more things

> *Too good to throw out.*
> Martin

and/or avoidance of discard and disposal. Steketee and Frost (2014a) propose that hoarding behaviours are reinforced either positively through positive emotional states or negatively reinforced in the short-term through avoidance of the negative emotional states associated with discard.

The formulation needs to pay particular attention to avoidance which may take the form of behavioural avoidance but can also include cognitive aspects of avoidance, such as deferring decision-making as a way of avoiding unpleasant emotions.

> *I'm hooked on these newspapers.*
> Danielle

A good formulation will demonstrate 'vicious cycles' of thoughts, feelings and behaviour and make the focus of intervention easily apparent to both therapist and client. The formulation model in Figure 1 has been criticised by some for the lack of attention paid to the perpetuating cycles commonly used in and familiar to most UK practitioners of CBT.

Bream (2013) and colleagues at the Centre for Anxiety Disorders and Trauma at the Maudsley Hospital, London, have developed the 'vicious shamrock' model (see Figure 2) to overcome this. In the vicious shamrock, the clutter has a central role. Three main sets of beliefs are included: beliefs about acquiring, discarding and 'stuckness'. Each of these beliefs has its own set of maintaining factors, and all beliefs reinforce and in turn are maintained by the presence of the clutter. All the components of the Steketee and Frost model are included.

The vicious shamrock (Figure 2) is a work in progress; clinicians are encouraged to work creatively with it and emphasise whichever elements of the model are most useful to the client (rather than insist on filling all the boxes). A formal evaluation of the model is planned.

> *Somebody will want it.*
> Martin

COGNITIONS

The CB model suggests the importance of thoughts in perpetuating or maintaining the problem. The thoughts can be many and varied, but are not always easily accessible to the person. Unlike in OCD where thoughts are characterised as intrusive and distressing, the thoughts experienced by the person who hoards may not be upsetting or anxiety provoking, but can appear reasonable and appropriate. Examples might include 'I just need more storage space' or 'throwing things away is bad for the environment'. Other thoughts such as 'if I throw it away I might regret it', or 'I need to organise it perfectly or not bother at all' may be more open to debate. Identifying negative automatic thoughts will allow exploration of alternatives, or costs and benefits of thinking this way.

Figure 2: The vicious shamrock model (Bream, 2013).

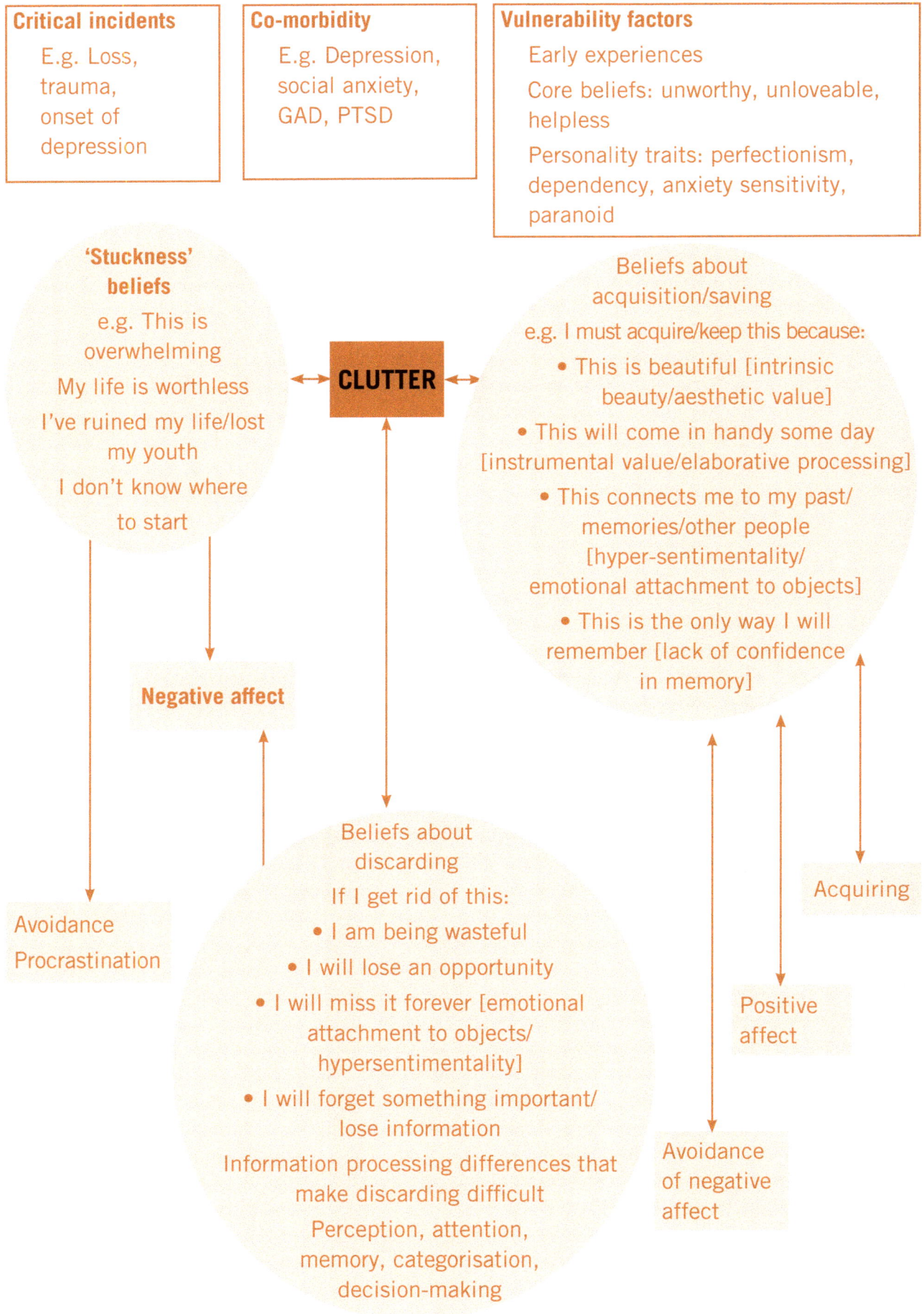

Critical incidents	Co-morbidity	Vulnerability factors
E.g. Loss, trauma, onset of depression	E.g. Depression, social anxiety, GAD, PTSD	Early experiences Core beliefs: unworthy, unloveable, helpless Personality traits: perfectionism, dependency, anxiety sensitivity, paranoid

'Stuckness' beliefs

e.g. This is overwhelming

My life is worthless

I've ruined my life/lost my youth

I don't know where to start

CLUTTER

Beliefs about acquisition/saving

e.g. I must acquire/keep this because:

• This is beautiful [intrinsic beauty/aesthetic value]

• This will come in handy some day [instrumental value/elaborative processing]

• This connects me to my past/memories/other people [hyper-sentimentality/emotional attachment to objects]

• This is the only way I will remember [lack of confidence in memory]

Negative affect

Avoidance Procrastination

Beliefs about discarding

If I get rid of this:

• I am being wasteful

• I will lose an opportunity

• I will miss it forever [emotional attachment to objects/hypersentimentality]

• I will forget something important/lose information

Information processing differences that make discarding difficult

Perception, attention, memory, categorisation, decision-making

Acquiring

Positive affect

Avoidance of negative affect

Strong attachment to items interferes with the ability to discard. People may be very attached to possessions that have personal meaning, giving them particular value. Kellett et al. (2010) identified three main types of value:

- **intrinsic value** – something that is of itself valuable, e.g. foreign currency;

- **instrumental value** – the value in being able to make future use of an item, e.g. old clothes that could be used to repair other clothes, items that can be recycled; and

- **sentimental value** – the affect associated with a possessions, e.g. old photos, diaries, or albums, as they signify or represent parts of the self, that may act as reminders of a person's life, or relationships with others.

> *I am appalled by the sight of neighbours' rubbish bins overflowing with refuse. Where is this 'away' that we discard to? Mars?*
>
> Harry

A strong desire not to damage the environment further may contribute to difficulties with disposal. Many people with hoarding problems have high commitment to repairing, re-using and recycling things. In some cases, value may be less strongly attached to the items themselves, but more strongly attached to places that are used for landfill.

It may be that it is rigidity and lack of flexibility in adhering to beliefs that maintains the problem. Steketee and Frost (2014a) noted that many of the thoughts expressed can be held by all, but most people can weigh up whether it's useful to continue thinking you could sell an item, if you have never in the past 20 years actually done so. Hartl et al.

> *If I throw this away – journals, diaries – I won't remember things like what I was actually doing at that stage of my life.*
>
> Christine

(2004) identified a greater tendency amongst people who hoard to report a more catastrophic misinterpretation of the results of forgetting. In addition they found a lower self-reported confidence in their memory.

Exploration of beliefs about the importance of the need to remember or knowing information about the item can be crucial. For some people, beliefs may include the need to retain the physical object, to facilitate the act of remembering. Some people are relatively happy to dispose of things they have checked, but the checking behaviour itself can become another aspect of a general pattern of avoidance.

Meta-cognitions appear, as in anxiety problems, to be key in addressing hoarding difficulties.

People may be attached to possessions that have personal meaning.

INFORMATION-PROCESSING DIFFICULTIES

The information processing abilities of people diagnosed with hoarding disorder is an area of debate. It has been suggested that information-processing deficits play a more significant role for people with hoarding difficulties than for people with other mental health problems or matched controls (McMillan et al., 2013). Samuels et al. (2007) describe people with hoarding difficulties as having greater difficulty with indecision and with initiating or completing tasks. A study by Hartl et al. (2004) found people with hoarding difficulties recalled less information on delayed recall, and used less effective organisational strategies. McMillan et al. (2013) found people who hoard had significantly greater perseveration errors and deficits in processing information. They identified problems which would interfere with the ability to form effective strategies, problems in concept formation and impulsivity. Difficulties in sustaining attention were associated with increased severity in hoarding difficulties. McMillan et al. (2013) also found people had greater difficulty responding appropriately to feedback, that is, changing their strategy in response to ineffectiveness.

> *You doubt your ability to make decisions.*
> Harry

> *As my house is disorganised, so too is my mind.*
> Harry

Mackin et al.'s (2011) study compared people with long-standing depression, some of whom also had hoarding difficulties. Despite both groups having depression they found the hoarding group had significant difficulties in categorisation and problem-solving. They also found clinically significant impairment on information processing and verbal memory, suggesting that some neuropsychological impairment is specific to people with hoarding problems.

> *What's difficult is my organisational skills: cooking is hard, things get all out of sync ... you have to be very strict with yourself.*
> Danielle

It has been suggested that executive dysfunction seen among people with hoarding difficulties will impact on the ability to sort and organise possessions, increase the tendency to see each item as unique, and therefore finding it hard to group items together, or find similarities between items. However, further research is needed to identify the relationship between hoarding behaviour and neuropsychological functioning. It is not clear whether hoarding behaviour, or simply living in highly cluttered environments, leads to deficits, or whether the deficits predispose people to develop a problem with hoarding.

> *You don't want to do it because you don't want to make mistakes.*
> Danielle

Some subtle neurocognitive deficits, including difficulties with categorisation, decision-making and memory have been suggested to be associated with hoarding behaviour across the life-span (e.g. Grisham et al., 2007; Grisham et al., 2010; Hartl et al., 2004; Wincze et al., 2007). Some of these neurocognitive deficits may naturally worsen with increasing age (Deary et al., 2009). There is also the possibility that cognitive impairment is indicative of a dementia process, which in itself is sometimes associated with hoarding behaviour (Hwang et al.,1998).

Glenhill et al. (2021) analysed previous studies that indicated that people with a diagnosis of hoarding disorder have, as a group, some impairments in attention, working memory, organisation, planning/problem-solving, visuospatial learning, and memory. They stress that the most robust findings are around attention and organisation. Notably, these are both problems for people with ADHD, a condition that often co-occurs with problems with hoarding.

However, not all results are in accordance with the hypothesis that people with hoarding have specific deficits. Woody et al. (2021) found that there were no reliable cognitive differences between people with hoarding problems and control groups. They suggest that the cognitive abilities may be intact, but it is the person's appraisal of their abilities, their confidence in them, that may need addressing, rather than the need for cognitive remediation therapy for actual skill deficits. This position is supported by the meta-analysis of Stumpf et al. (2023) who found that only categorisation skills were different, and that too could be confidence in those skills rather than actual ability. They found no impairments between people with a diagnosis of hoarding disorder and controls in relation to attention, episodic memory, working memory, information-processing speed, planning, decision-making, inhibitory control, mental flexibility, language, and visuospatial ability. This is definitely an area where more research is necessary, and has implications for the design of interventions.

BEHAVIOUR

Avoidance of disposal, or anything associated with it, serves to maintain the problem with hoarding. Disposal can trigger anxiety, but successful avoidance over many years can mask the underlying fear and lead to the problem being described as 'lack of time' or 'lack of space to sort'.

> *You keep them and then you can't find them.*
> Danielle

Difficulties can arise from avoidance of a whole range of things in addition to disposal. The person may avoid opening post or dealing with usual household activities such as paying bills, washing clothes, returning calls or cleaning up.

People sometimes attempt sorting but begin 'churning'. This is a term used to describe moving things from one place to another. It may seem as if the person is actively engaged in sorting and disposal, but if their actions are assessed in

> *You keep kicking yourself about what you haven't done.*
> Danielle

detail, it becomes clear that the sorting or disposal is minimal. This behaviour is actually a type of avoidance.

Avoidance of seeking help is also commonly seen among people who hoard. The avoidance of contact with any other people (or specifically those that might suggest help is required) can exacerbate the difficulties in engaging in treatment.

Avoidance may take the form of complaining about the interference of external agencies, such as housing support staff or social care. Additionally, for some an excessive preoccupation with 'the reasons why' can prevent working behaviourally. As in other mental health difficulties, people can describe waiting until they feel right before tackling the difficulty, rather than working on it despite how it feels.

EMOTIONS

A key aspect of the CB model is to ascertain the role and function of the emotions that the person that hoards experiences around their possessions, when planning discard,

> *I think it's to do with anger... anger is the bottom line of this little lot.*
> Danielle

at the point of discard and following discard. As described, it may be that the behaviours serve the function of avoiding negative emotional states such as anxiety. A central component is, therefore, to understand how the person who hoards might also avoid positive and negative emotions.

Grisham et al. (2005) showed people who hoard endorse significantly less anxiety, worry, stress and negative affect than those with OCD. In addition to the tendency to experience less negative emotional affect, people with hoarding difficulties tend to have difficulties forming emotional attachments with other people (Medard & Kellett, 2014). It is not entirely clear if the difficulty in forming emotional attachments precedes the development of hoarding, or if hoarding behaviour leads to an avoidance of close emotional relationships as a means of coping with shame, embarrassment and other consequences of their behaviour.

Kellett and Holden (2014) evaluated the evidence for emotional attachment to objects and its role in hoarding. Moderate quality evidence indicated that hoarders have stronger emotional attachment to objects than both clinical and non-clinical populations. Associated effect sizes were large, suggesting that emotional attachment to objects is an important construct within hoarding.

> *I tend to have controlling behaviour. Some of my hoarding feels as if it relates to loss of control.*
> Harry

A review of previous research into emotional regulation and hoarding by Barton et al. (2021) has some interesting findings and implications. They found that hoarding is associated with restricted emotional understanding, emotion avoidance, limited mood management strategies, and behaviour regulation problems related to emotions. If this is the case, then this sets an agenda for intervention along a different line to the information processing deficit approaches.

Part of the challenge for people with hoarding problems may be managing the uncomfortable emotions that can be generated by making decisions about one's things and discarding some of them. Tolin et al. (2018) found that people diagnosed with hoarding disorder reported higher levels of problems with emotional regulation than controls. This has been supported by other studies, such as Taylor et al. (2018), who, in a qualitative study of a small sample of people with a diagnosis of hoarding disorder, found themes of problems in identifying feelings, negative attitudes to emotional experience, avoidance strategies and problems with emotional regulation. These findings have implications for the skills learning offered as part of treatment packages for people with problems with hoarding. Teaching distress tolerance and emotional regulation could be valuable skills to learn.

ATTACHMENT

Attachment theory (Bowlby 1969/82; Ainsworth, 1978) is an obvious candidate to explore in relation to hoarding. The formation of strong attachments to objects and a subsequent response of emotional distress when discard would be normative is a key feature of hoarding disorder. According to Mathes et al. (2020) objects may be a substitute for secure relationships and offer a source of comfort. People turn to objects for comfort when people let them down. There is a growing body of evidence that hoarding disorder is associated with an insecure attachment style (David et al., 2022). Chia et al. (2021) have found a complex interaction between traumatic events and early home environment, the attachment style highlighted being an insecure one.

FAMILY HISTORY

There appears to be a tendency for hoarding to run in families, occurring more frequently in relatives of those with OCD and hoarding, than in just OCD. Samuels et al.'s study (2002) of 126 people with OCD showed 12 per cent of people with hoarding difficulties had a first-degree relative with hoarding difficulties, compared with 3 per cent of people with a diagnosis of OCD but not hoarding. Iervolino et al. (2009) completed a study of 5,022 twins and found 2.3 per cent of them met caseness for hoarding, with a significantly higher rate for male twins (4.1 per cent) than female twins (2.1 per cent).

> *My parents had hoarding tendencies... they were born in 1914 and lived through hard times when it often wasn't possible to get a replacement. They farmed on a very limited budget and were very good at re-using things.*
>
> Harry

A CASE EXAMPLE USING A CBT APPROACH

Maria is a 39-year-old woman who was born in Portugal. As a child she lived with her parents until she was five and was then cared for by her grandmother when her parents moved to Britain. She moved to the UK age 12 and learnt English but struggled at school, leaving with few qualifications. She worked as a health-care assistant before meeting her husband whom she married aged 25. They had two children, but when she was pregnant with the youngest he left her and she has had no contact since.

Maria remembers beginning her collection of soft cuddly toys as a child, and finding it difficult generally to get rid of old toys as she wanted to keep reminders of her parents. After moving to live with her parents she had frequent conflict with them as she was unwilling to let anything be thrown away. Her first home with her husband was cluttered but after he left it became quite overwhelming. She found it hard not to visit charity shops, initially to buy children's clothes and toys, but increasingly her purchases extended to clothes she thought they would 'grow into', household objects that 'might come in useful' and soft toys that she described as 'I can't leave them alone in the shop, they should be in a home'. She also found it hard to get rid of papers, household bills, flyers, receipts and statements. Her home became increasingly difficult to live in, slowly all the surfaces were piled high, the floor was completely covered in storage boxes of toys, piles of papers, and amongst furniture that was either broken waiting for repair, or being used for storage. Thinking of disposing papers led to Maria feeling anxious because she worried that 'I'll forget to pay a bill, and get cut off, or worse, evicted' although she hadn't actually got behind with rent or her bills.

Her health visitor expressed concern about her care of the children, and tried to support her to clear space so the children could play. After many attempts at clearing, Maria was extremely anxious, and thoughts about the soft toys being thrown away, increased her thoughts that 'I'm such a bad person – I've allowed all those toys to go to landfill' 'those toys would give some poor child pleasure, and I've thrown them away' . Maria had regular visual intrusive images of soft toys in the bin. Eventually, social services became involved, so worried about the impact of the home on the children's wellbeing and safety that they were placed in foster care. She continued to hope that one day she will get 'on top of it' and they will come back to live with her.

Maria reluctantly agreed to see the clinical psychologist, thinking it was a waste of time as she had had help to clear her home many times, and it had always led to her feeling very anxious and overwhelmed. This led to her acquiring even more toys, often from well meaning neighbours, who thought she would make use of them, or from charity shops.

The clinical psychologist spent time building trust, and offering hope that change is possible if they worked at Maria's pace. They collaboratively worked on agreeing a goal with Maria. She found it hard to prioritise, and her children's social worker had instructed her to 'make it suitable' for the children. Her clinical psychologist worked with them both to establish the minimum steps required in order that her children could visit. They began by working in the kitchen to make space to allow food to be stored in the fridge and easy access to the fridge and cooker. They developed together a list of 'rules' about where things should go while sorting. Maria was encouraged to do behavioural work in short, regular periods of time, without spending too long deciding on any one item. She sometimes found herself simply moving boxes from one place to another, and sessions were arranged at home to practice disposal. She began by throwing away broken toys, and food that was past its use by date. This graded approach to addressing her avoidance helped Maria learn about how her anxiety about throwing things away led to difficulties with disposal.

After building up some trust in her clinical psychologist, she began to explore and test out some of her beliefs about the importance of remembering, leading to some reappraisal and decatastrophising 'forgetting'. It emerged that her biggest fear was that others would 'think I'm stupid'. In the past, Maria had avoided not just discarding old or broken items, but also avoided talking about her feelings about losing her children by saying to anyone who asked 'It's only temporary, when I get sorted they will come back'.

Maria found it difficult to spend time at home, feeling very low and overwhelmed by thoughts such as 'I am a terrible mother to allow this to happen'. She distracted herself by walking round all the charity shops every day, and bringing home more things. The soft toys led to increased feelings of pleasure and thoughts such as 'I can give this one a good home' or 'this teddy would be a lovely present for someone'. She developed a strong identity as someone who cared about others and looked after others, while at the same time finding it hard to care for herself.

Developing a shared formulation allowed Maria to have an understanding of why she found disposal so difficult, and encouraged her to show herself the care that she so easily showed to others. The role of avoidance in keeping things the same, preventing change was addressed, and Maria began noticing where she was 'avoiding' rather than experiencing emotions, and learning to manage the discomfort.

When working on sorting and discarding, Maria became quite easily distracted, worrying about losing one of her soft toys, and searching for it, while in the middle of sorting household paperwork. On discovering old soft toys, she became consumed with thoughts of how the toy might have felt being lost, and said she was unable to part with any of them despite most being in a very poor state of repair. The hierarchy of items she could dispose of enabled her to work at her own pace, and feel in control about the decisions being made. It was important that this list was Maria's and the clinical psychologist kept the focus on what was needed to happen to enable the children to visit.

Maria continued to build confidence in her ability to throw things away, or at least donate to charity shops, she started taking a bag of papers with her every time she left the house to put in the recycling bins. Once the kitchen was partially cleared, discussion with the social worker led to Maria being supported to have her visits with the children in her home. This further increased Maria's confidence, and she began clearing their bedroom in the hope that they may be able to stay overnight in the future.

Statutory powers

There may come a time when services (or carers) consider forcibly intervening, particularly if children or other vulnerable adults are adversely affected by the behaviour of those caring for them. In working with adults who hoard, it is essential to consider the wellbeing, development and welfare of children (DfES, 2003). Although the children may not be known to services, the responsibility to consider their needs is everyone's (DoH, 2013). It is particularly important to have joined-up working, consistently liaising with GPs, schools and social-care services. If the needs of children are being compromised, then policies and guidance for safeguarding children in need should be followed (BPS, 2014a).

MENTAL HEALTH LEGISLATION

Use of Mental Health Act (MHA) legislation may be considered, either for assessment or treatment. The Mental Health Act 1983 (which was substantially amended in 2007) is the law in England and Wales that allows people with a 'mental disorder' (i.e. any disability or disorder of the mind) to be admitted to hospital, detained and treated without their consent. This is either for their own health and safety, or for the protection of other people. Scotland and Northern Ireland have their own laws about compulsory treatment for mental ill health.

Whereas the 1983 MHA focused on strengthening patients' rights to seek independent reviews of their treatment, the 2007 MHA is largely focused on public protection and risk management.

ENVIRONMENTAL HEALTH LEGISLATION

If the person who hoards has rubbish leaking or spilling into neighbouring property, smells emanating from or rats living among their things, then environmental health departments have recourse to legal powers.

The Prevention of Damage by Pests Act 1949 can be used but only if there is visible sight of rats. Alternatively, under the Public Health Act 1936 or the Prevention of Damage by Pests Act 1949, a 'threat of disease' or 'nuisance' can be used to get a warrant to enter and can lead to compulsory clearing and/or removal from the home.

MENTAL CAPACITY LEGISLATION

The Mental Capacity Act 2005 implemented in 2007, provides a statutory framework to empower and protect vulnerable people who are not able to make their own decisions. This Act makes clear who can take decisions, in which situations, and how they should go about this. In 2006, the BPS published guidance in relation to this Act for practitioner psychologists in England and Scotland. In Scotland legislation for mental capacity came earlier with the Adults with Incapacity (Scotland) Act 2000. There is no mental capacity legislation in Northern Ireland and so these issues are dealt with under common law.

The key principles enshrined in the Act are:

- a presumption of capacity – every adult has the right to make his/her own decisions and must be assumed to have capacity to do so unless it is proved otherwise;
- the right for individuals to be supported to make their own decisions – people must be given all appropriate help before anyone concludes that they cannot make their own decisions;

- that individuals must retain the right to make what might be seen to be an unwise decision;
- that anything done for or on behalf of people without capacity must be in their best interests; and
- that anything done for or on behalf of people without capacity should be the least restrictive of their basic rights and freedoms.
- A person engaged in extreme hoarding behaviour could, under the Mental Capacity Act 2005, be considered suitable for a Capacity assessment.
- Section 2 of the MCA states that a person lacks capacity if they cannot decide at the material time due to an impairment or disturbance in mind or brain functioning. Hoarding Disorder can be considered such an impairment or disturbance.
- Section 3 of the MCA states that the person cannot make the decision and therefore lacks capacity if they are unable to i) Understand information relevant to the decision, ii) retain the information, iii) balance the information in deciding, iv) communicate their decision by speech, sign language or another way.
- Capacity assessment for hoarding, as all capacity assessments, must relate to a specific issue that the person needs to decide on at a particular time. In the case of hoarding, this could be about accommodation, a tenancy, a care package or accepting help.
- Capacity assessments should be carried out at the earliest possible opportunity, and the decision-making process of the assessor should be documented with the time and the specific decision clearly stated.

SAFEGUARDING ADULTS

An adult at risk is defined by the Department of Health as:

> a person aged 18 years or over, who is or may be in need of community care services by reason of mental or other disability, age or illness; and who is or may be unable to take care of him or herself, or unable to protect him or herself against significant harm or exploitation.

> No Secrets Guidance (DoH, 2000)

In March 2011, the Law Commission recommended that the term 'vulnerable adult' was replaced by 'adult at risk' because the term vulnerable adult may wrongly imply that some of the fault for the abuse (harm) lies with the adult being abused (harmed). It is important to note that people with capacity can also be at risk.

The degree of risk is determined by a range of interconnecting factors including personal characteristics, factors associated with their situation or environment and social factors. Risk needs to be assessed in terms of how able vulnerable adults are to make and exercise their own informed choices free from duress, pressure or undue influence of any sort, and to protect themselves from abuse (harm), neglect and exploitation.

In Scotland, The Adult Support and Protection (Scotland) Act 2007 was passed to protect people who are unable to safeguard their own interests as a result of disability or mental disorder.

The Care Act 2014 introduced new responsibilities and duties for local authorities in England. The Act is clear that self-neglect is a form of abuse, and hoarding behaviours can be considered as self-neglect. In practice, this means that a person's hoarding may trigger a safeguarding investigation. The Act has led to the development of hoarding frameworks and hoarding boards, so a multi-agency approach can be taken to assess and manage risk.

DIFFICULTIES IN BRINGING STATUTORY POWERS TO BEAR

The issues with using statutory powers are many, not least the fact that forcible treatment can be an extremely traumatic process for the person involved. Use of mental health legislative powers to remove a person forcibly, followed by wholesale house clearance, rarely lead to resolution of hoarding difficulties. People describe feeling violated and distraught at the loss of control, valued possessions and self-efficacy. Forcible psychological treatment is unlikely to facilitate collaboration and development of the good therapeutic relationship essential to helping people who hoard deal with their situation.

Psychological therapies and interventions

Part 4: Psychological therapies and interventions

Key points

It is critical to remain non-judgemental and create a positive working alliance when dealing with people who hoard, often in the face of stuttering and slow progress.

The most effective approach may be to work towards improving quality of life despite mental health difficulties, rather than symptom change.

Effective interventions include individual CBT, motivational work, and group and family interventions.

The value of reflective practice

In any area of clinical work, it is useful for the practitioner psychologist to be a reflective practitioner, and as part of their reflections to be mindful of their own values and beliefs regarding help provision. This is particularly pertinent when working with people who hoard, as many of our beliefs and assumptions about how a person should live can influence assessment outcomes.

It is important to recognise the value of the possessions the person may have built up over time, while at the same time acknowledging potential risks. The process of change is more likely to set off on the right foot if the person feels understood, and their objects are treated with respect.

Quality of life and recovery versus 'cure'

The importance of reducing risks, such as fire, health concerns and accidents, may be the primary motivating force for change rather than stopping or extinguishing hoarding behaviours. While the person might not appreciate the need to increase discard, they may understand the risks of precariously balanced items that might topple over and hurt them or others. They may see this as an issue that is worth trying to deal with. The motivation to address safety concerns

> *It was necessary to make a firm decision about change, stop acquiring unnecessary possessions and declutter my mind.*
> Danielle

may be helped by leverage applied from other sources, such as the threat of eviction or threat of children being removed. We may need to work towards improving quality of life despite mental health difficulties and define precisely what really is manageable change. Finding out what values the person holds dear, what they want their life to look like socially, at work and for themselves and their family, may be a way of engaging them in change that does not lead to head-on conflict. Working with change that is possible and achievable, and maintaining any changes made, is just as important as thinking treatment will remove the hoarding problem.

Individual therapy

MOTIVATIONAL WORK

Ambivalence about the benefits of change can sometimes be confused with lack of insight (Steketee & Frost, 2014a). It needs to be recognised that motivation depends not only on the discrepancy between how life is and how the person wants it to be, but also on having confidence that change is possible. It may be that after a long struggle to 'get on top of things', people who present as if 'lacking insight' may actually be struggling with eroded confidence and doubts about whether their attempts to organise will work. Steketee and Frost (2014a) suggest that this may lead to them reducing the discrepancy by changing their appraisal of their current situation rather than continuing (and failing) to change their behaviour.

Practitioner psychologists may want to consider cycle of change concepts in relation to referrals in terms of whether the person who hoards is pre-contemplative of change, contemplative of change or ready to change their hoarding behaviours (Prochaska & DiClemente, 1983). Although the role of motivational interviewing is recognised but currently under-researched in hoarding, practitioner psychologists should be able to spot and make use of any change talk exhibited by the person who hoards (Steketee & Frost, 2007).

COGNITIVE BEHAVIOUR THERAPY

Steketee and Frost have written a useful therapist guide (2014a) and workbook (2014b) that can potentially be given to the person to use themselves. The use of Socratic questioning and 'downward arrow' can be helpful to identity negative automatic thoughts and core beliefs.

One specific strategy relating to hoarding is a process by which the person simply talks about the object, rather than engaging in 'restructuring thoughts'. Steketee and Frost (2014a) demonstrate that a disposal rate similar to that achieved by those without hoarding difficulties can be encouraged if the person spends time talking about their possessions first. Therapy may also include identifying values, imaginal work, practising key skills such as sorting and decision-making, thought-listing and habituation exercises.

Therapy needs to include the strengthening of problem-solving skills, reducing acquisition, and exposure tasks. It is important that practitioner psychologists avoid persuasion, as this can lead to further strengthening of beliefs that disposal is unnecessary.

Adaptations to therapy for people with cognitive impairments have been described by Rossiter and Holmes (2013), and many practitioner psychologists will be familiar with the needs of people with additional difficulties or disabilities. Intervention to attenuate the hoarding should be based on the functional assessment and aim at achieving a balance between the ego-syntonic function

> I find sorting and discarding very stressful and tiring, so can only manage a limited amount at a time.
>
> Harry

> You've got to be prepared to do the work. I've tried hard to cut down on what I bring in.
>
> Danielle

> I had sessions of CBT… I found this useful in questioning my automatic assumptions about things. Simply to ask 'is this so?' can be very powerful technique in changing my behaviour.
>
> Anon

of the hoarding behaviour and the needs of families and carers. In some cases, this may take the form of teaching new skills, for example about exchange, money and shopping, to enable the person to obtain and use materials in a more appropriate manner. Given the ego-syntonic nature of much hoarding by people with ASC, an intervention based on controlling the collection may be the most appropriate option. This might involve setting up a system by which the person donates, for example, a pair of shoes to charity on a weekly basis before purchasing a new pair for their collection.

Staff, carers and practitioner psychologists may conceptualise the work as a linear process not unlike a house renovation project. Sorting and disposal might be imagined as work that ebbs and flows but generally once the decision has been made, it progresses in a steady manner towards clearance.

In reality, clearance may progress and then return to a previous state of clutter, or even worsen, before moving towards renewed attempts at clearance. Recognition of the process of behavioural change can assist in remaining empathic when the pace of change seems stuttering or very slow (Miller & Rollnick, 2013).

LARGE CLEAR-OUT SESSIONS

People presenting to services have often already experienced major clear outs. This will increase their fears about therapy and reduce their motivation to make changes. Forced clearances may change the living environment temporarily but are unlikely to lead to behaviour change. Steketee and Frost (2014a) specifically warn against this strategy and stress the impact which may be traumatic for the person. If a person is already engaged in sessions with support staff attempting to clear and sort, practitioner psychologist needs to be aware of the tension between working at a manageable pace for the individual while appearing to 'slow down' the work carried out by others. It can be helpful to identify rules for sorting or disposing and draw these up with the person. These can then be shared with friends or others.

Harry describes his strategy

I found the following helpful in sorting out a kitchen cupboard and the garden shed:

- Completely empty the space and pile the contents elsewhere.
- Clean it and leave to dry out.
- Return items that 'should be there' in an ordered way.
- Discard useless items off the premises ASAP.
- Return remaining items to where they belong, if possible, or box up and store them for later organising.
- Work on a discrete, limited area; end the session with as little extra 'mess' as is practical.
- Accept that it will be disruptive, hard work and you will take time to get used to the new system; do only as many areas as feels comfortable within a short period. I find that it is easier to do a bit, then keep it going, then do another bit, and so on.

These are habits that I've had for most of my life; changing them for better ones will be hard.

HELP FOR CO-PRESENTING DIFFICULTIES

People with problems with hoarding often have another presenting difficulty; high rates of depression and anxiety have been found (Frost et al., 2011) and ADHD (Grassi et al., 2023). It is therefore vital to enable the person to find help for these. Whilst hoarding is a condition in its own right and successfully dealing with the person's other problems will not resolve the hoarding, not addressing the other person's other problem will reduce the likelihood of being able to affect change with the hoarding. For example, if a person is clinically depressed, the effects of that depression may affect their ability to carry out tasks to address the hoarding as they lack the motivation to do so. Though a mental health service may consider that hoarding disorder is not within the services they provide, the other problems that the person has may be within the service provision. Significant physical health problems are often co-presenting, and help for these should be sought, including any psychological approach, where appropriate.

IDENTITY AND VALUES

The tendency to self-identify with the mental health difficulty you struggle with can hold benefits but also bring with it significant problems. The implication of passivity and lack of control in holding a diagnostic descriptor as one's identity is clear.

> *The idea of it being helpful to see hoarding as a 'behavioural difficulty' rather than 'part of the self' rings true to me.*
> Harry

Therefore, identification as a mother or a musician rather than a hoarder is an important shift for people to make. Kellett et al. (2010) describe the common experience of fusion between self and possessions in people who hoard and discuss the importance of 'identity shift'. Seeing the hoarding as a 'behavioural difficulty' rather than locating it as part of the self therefore increases self-efficacy and options for change.

Self-help support groups

Increasingly, groups are being set up around the country to work specifically with people who have hoarding difficulties. This has immediate benefits in reducing the sense of isolation and shame associated with hoarding.

> *We are extremely lucky that we have a group and a group that is set up in a very supportive way. How many people have that?*
> Christine

A growing number of self-help groups have been established around the country. One of the first to be set up was in Surrey, co-facilitated by workers in the local mental health NHS trust, a local mental health charity and a carer (Holmes et al., 2014). The group runs monthly, is well attended and regularly includes psycho-education, personal testimonies and setting of personal goals. Other groups are now running as far and wide in the UK as Edinburgh, Plymouth, Gateshead, Kettering and London.

A more structured approach to self-help groups called the Buried in Treasures Workshop has been developed in America, with resources and a book to guide facilitators (Frost et al., 2011c; Frost et al., 2012). The structured workshops run for 13 weeks. They are facilitated by non-professionals and held in non-mental- health settings. The dropout rate has been reported to be 10 per cent for these groups which, given the engagement difficulties for this population, is very encouraging and early indications are that this approach is as effective as CBT-based groups (Tolin et al., 2014, Delucchi et al, 2019).

There is a difference in the approach and philosophy between purely support groups for HD and those support groups that have a treatment orientation. In a HD support group, attendees are encouraged to express their emotions and to provide each other with encouragement and validation. In the treatment-oriented HD support groups, then a much greater emphasis is placed on the need for change and change is therefore facilitated. Most of the evidence base concerns treatment-oriented HD support groups and these interventions have been developed and conceived as 'low intensity' HD interventions.

> *I have found the group beneficial as it has provided a non-confrontational place to learn and face this problem.*
>
> Danielle

A drawback of individual and group psychological interventions for HD is that often lengthy interventions are needed, these are labour intensive and also require high levels of training and ongoing supervision. Akin to other low intensity interventions, treatment-oriented HD support groups are brief, use a workbook approach, lack any domiciliary visits and are facilitated by non-professional staff that occupy the role of coach as opposed to therapist. The associated workbook that has been developed and is used in these groups is called *Buried in Treasures; Help for Compulsive Acquiring, Saving and Hoarding* (Tolin, Frost & Steketee, 2007). The evidence base for treatment-oriented HD support groups is still under development. This evidence base also suggests that this style of intervention can be effective when used in a stepped-care style of approach where the individuals' needs and readiness to change are matched to the style and intensity of the approach. For example, Frost, Pekareva-Kochergina and Maxner (2011) conducted two studies with 13-week treatment-oriented HD support groups to suggest that this low intensity HD treatment held promise.

When compared to a waitlist control, then treatment-oriented HD support groups show a significant reduction in HD symptoms (Frost, Ruby & Shuer, 2012). When compared to an active control, then treatment-oriented HD support groups have been shown to be less efficacious than group CBT for HD (Muroff, Steketee, Bratiotis & Ross, 2012). The role of treatment-oriented HD support groups therefore can be considered when (1) they can be offered as an adjunct to individual psychological therapy, (2) as a frontline intervention for mild HD cases that are motivated and ready to change, (3) as an alternative to individual psychological therapy when this treatment is inaccessible and (4) as a remote and internet delivered intervention.

ONLINE SUPPORT

There is a wealth of information available online to support work with people who hoard, the person themselves and their relatives. Making recommendations can be challenging because applications, websites and other sources of good support change rapidly or become out of date, and good governance is difficult to establish. It is worth exploring online, with the proviso of approaching some of the less effective strategies marketed as 'psychological treatment' with caution.

Working with carers and family members

People who respond well to treatment tend to have carer involvement, as this can increase motivation for change. The needs or hopes of relatives can be used as motivating factors, or work can be supported by involving them in practical support around clearing. It is now well established that carers have rights to services in their own right (DoH, 2014), and that living alongside someone with a severe mental health difficulty has a significant impact on the carer.

> *My daughters would not have friends in and things because of the way the house was, it affected life in a big way.*
> Anon

One of the issues is that, while many partners and children of people who hoard will be hugely affected by living in a house that has restricted access or is not usable for usual purposes, they may not see themselves as a 'carer'. The guiding principle of reaching out to people in relationships with those who hoard must be one of reducing distress, whether they share a house or are frequent visitors (as might be the case with adult children). The question of the effectiveness of services that focus solely on the individual rather than the family or wider community needs to be carefully considered.

Storch et al. (2011a) describe specific needs in working with young people who hoard and the essential involvement of parents, to increase their agency in targeting behaviour termed as disruptive. Burton et al. (2015) state that it is essential to study and intervene with children and adolescents with hoarding behaviours as this is the age when the problem often first begins; it has the potential to continue into adulthood and can affect psychological and social wellbeing in several ways. This is echoed by Whomsley (2020), who stressed the need to develop ways to help children and adolescents have healthy relationships with their things, be they physical or digital.

Steketee (1993) found that empathy and positive interactions with significant others of the person with hoarding problems were linked with the maintenance of positive progression following behavioural treatment for OCD. A belief by significant others that the person could control their OCD, as well as criticism and anger, were correlated with relapse at follow-up 6–14 months after treatment. These results suggest that families may require psycho-education in order to better understand mental health problems, and that families of those with difficulties with hoarding should be included in the treatment process and offered therapeutic support of their own. Chasson et al. (2014) have shown promising results from training offered to relatives to improve their skills as motivators. This not only enabled family members to improve their coping skills but also increased hopefulness.

Multidisciplinary working and working with other agencies

Working with people with hoarding problems within an health and social care service can utilise the skills of all the disciplines within a team, a multidisciplinary approach. This can utilise a case management approach and be organised as a pathway. In addition, working with people with hoarding problems can involve working with a range of agencies beyond health and social care.

The case management approach which has been widely used in mental health is one that can be applied to managing hoarding cases according to Bratiotis (2018). They examined the practices of community services for people with hoarding disorder in four cities in the USA who were mainly receiving a service that was involuntary for a hoarding disorder that was considered serious. They required interventions from several disciplines. What was offered could be placed on the headings of: case finding, supportive relationship, assessment, goal setting, brokerage, teaching/modelling, mentoring, advocacy and crisis intervention. A case management approach was taken in all four cities. This is not that surprising as people will be applying the models of working that they learned for working with complex cases for other mental health presentations. In the UK Tinlin-Dizon & Stephenson (2022) have developed multidisciplinary team (MDT) working into an MDT pathway for older adults with hoarding disorder. This has been developed to utilise the different skills of team members and to provide a model for best practice that can be copied elsewhere.

> *I also have a massive guilt trip when I leave the visit not having done anything in particular that has made a real difference – however small – because it feels like I have let him down and have not been much use at all.*
>
> A carer

An increased understanding of how and what to do in working with people who hoard whose behaviour is significantly impacting on family, neighbours or the wider community can only be of benefit. A joint approach among agencies may also ease the burden on all services. In some instances, this may simply mean acknowledging that everything possible has been tried, in other cases it may be essential to explain how psychological interventions cannot be 'imposed' or 'forced' on people.

Most housing support staff have little, if any, mental health experience and may view hoarding as simple but large house-clearance-type work. Without access to specialist help and guidance, it is likely that efforts to forcibly clear will result in the person being highly distressed and resume hoarding behaviours at the earliest opportunity (Grisham, 2011). Working in collaboration with practitioner psychologists to set achievable and specific goals can enhance both the process and the effects of the work of housing support staff.

Environmental health involvement can be used as a motivator for some people. Without any other clear reasons, the pressure of external agencies can be the only thing that leads someone to ask for help. However, environmental health services frequently struggle with how to proceed with working with people who hoard. Although in 65 per cent of environmental health work with people who hoard, mental health services are also involved (Holroyd & Price, 2009), this still leaves a large number where they are working alone or possibly with housing support services.

> *How to help without causing more upset?*
>
> A carer

The last ten years have seen multiagency working with people with hoarding problems develop organisation and cohesion. Across the country, different agencies, such as the fire service, housing, social care, health, and the police, have found that they were working with the hoarding problems of the same people in their region. Hoarding frameworks that outline a multiagency pathway to help the person with the problem and their community have been developed. The multiagency approach aims to improve communication, better manage risk, share information, and train and involve the person with hoarding problems in decision-making.

Organised multiagency working will likely be a crucial part of the services offered to people with hoarding problems in the future. In a paper titled: 'In an ideal world, that would be a multiagency service because you need everybody's expertise.' Haighton et al. (2023) suggest that this service would be psychology-led.

NICE, BPS and other guidance

The NHS Choices website recommends CBT as the treatment of choice for hoarding (NHS, 2014). People working with those who hoard should also consider the guidance produced by their own organisations, which is likely to cover risk management, health and safety of staff and working with other agencies.

The guidance contained in this set of good practice guidelines should be considered in conjunction with other relevant sets of BPS guidance, which include the following:

- DCP Good Practice Guidelines on the Use of Psychological Formulation (BPS, 2011)
  https://explore.bps.org.uk/content/report-guideline/bpsrep.2011.rep100
- DCP Policy on Supervision (BPS, 2014)
  https://explore.bps.org.uk/content/report-guideline/bpsrep.2014.inf224
- DCP Briefing Paper No 21: Clinical Psychologists and Assertive Outreach (BPS, 2013b)
  https://explore.bps.org.uk/content/report-guideline/bpsrep.2013.rep37
- BPS Guidance: 'What makes a good assessment of capacity' (2019),
  https://explore.bps.org.uk/content/report-guideline/bpsrep.2019.rep127
- BPS Guidance to help people making the decision of capacity: 'Supporting people who lack mental capacity: A guide to best interests decision making' (2021),
  https://explore.bps.org.uk/content/report-guideline/bpsrep.2022.inf149
- DCP Report on Understanding Psychosis and Schizophrenia (BPS, 2017)
  https://explore.bps.org.uk/content/report-guideline/bpsrep.2017.rep03
- DCP Position Statement on Classification of Behaviour and Experience in Relation to Functional Psychiatric Diagnoses – Time for a Paradigm Shift (BPS, 2013a).
  https://explore.bps.org.uk/content/report-guideline/bpsrep.2013.inf212

PART 5

Evaluation of how we are doing and future directions

Part 5: Evaluation of how we are doing and future directions

Key points

Further research, both in developing existing therapeutic approaches such as CBT, and in exploring potential new approaches, is required.

To ensure best practice, CPD, supervision and good governance are required.

Services need to have an understanding of the specific needs and difficulties for people with hoarding problems.

Effective interventions: a review of the evidence

CBT

The evaluation of CBT for hoarding difficulties includes qualitative case studies (Cermele et al., 2001; Shafran & Tallis, 1996) and single-case experimental designs (Hartl & Frost, 1999; Kellett, 2007; Pollock et al., 2014). The more rigorous single-case experimental studies all tend to show reduced hoarding and improved abilities to discard as a result of CBT in comparison with the baseline. Tolin et al. (2007) conducted an open trial of 26 sessions of CBT. While four out of 14 people dropped out of treatment, six out of 10 completing CBT were classed as 'treatment responders' using the SI-R. Ayers et al. (2011) applied the one-to-one CBT approach but in a sample of 12 older adult hoarders none dropped out of treatment. Results show that two of the people with hoarding difficulties actually worsened during treatment and only three could be classed as 'treatment responders' using the SI-R. The gains made by those people with hoarding problems who could make use of the CBT approach, were unfortunately not maintained at follow-up. Steketee et al. (2010) completed a wait-list control trial of individual CBT; nine people out of 46 dropped out of treatment. Improvement during CBT was statistically greater than the passive control of the wait-list across the hoarding outcome measures. A large effect size was evident and 41 per cent of completers were classed as 'treatment responders'.

Studies have tested the utility of CBT delivered in a group format. In the Steketee et al. (2000) study, six hoarders attended 15 two-hour group sessions, with statistically significant pre-post changes recorded on a modified Y-BOCS (Goodman et al., 1989). Muroff et al. (2009) delivered group CBT, with results showing modest (but statistically significant) pre-post treatment reductions. Gilliam et al. (2011) also assessed outcomes for group CBT. Significant pre-post group change was recorded, but nine of the 22 starters dropped out during treatment. Muroff et al. (2010) set out to test whether increased home-based assistance significantly improved the efficacy of group CBT. This was achieved by randomly allocating hoarders to one of three conditions: (a) 20-week group CBT (b) 20-week group CBT plus added home assistance and (c) a bibliotherapy control condition. Both the CBT groups showed significant pre-post treatment reductions, but with no apparent differences in terms of outcome between them. While the low-intensity approach of bibliotherapy was seen to be ineffective in changing hoarding behaviour in the Muroff et al. (2010) study, Pekareva-Kochergina and Frost (2009) found significant pre-post treatment reductions following a 13-week bibliotherapy group for hoarders.

Group CBT studies have been put through a meta-analysis by Bodryzlova et at. (2019). They made the following conclusions from their analysis: that there is strong evidence for the efficacy of group-based CBT, though the clinically significant change rate was low, protocols can be modified and extended, there is a need for controlled trials, and long-term follow-ups and a better understanding of hoarding disorder.

A meta-analysis of studies on CBT for hoarding disorder by Tolin et al. (2015) found that CBT significantly decreased hoarding-related behaviours, with the most potent effects on discarding behaviours. However, most participants still showed clinically significant hoarding behaviours after the intervention. Rogers et al. (2021) in a meta-analysis demonstrated the efficacy of CBT for hoarding disorder. Interestingly they also found that a larger number of female participants increased positive outcomes. Other variables such as modality (group or individual), home visits or not, did not moderate outcome. They point out the need for studies with controls.

Researchers have started to look at the mechanisms that maintain hoarding. A study by Levy et al. (2017) with 62 people with a diagnosis of hoarding disorder found that it was a change in saving cognitions that mediated change in acquisition, discard and clutter. Further studies with controls are needed to support these finding, but should they do so it would suggest that targeting belief change is key to improving hoarding problems. Tolin et al., (2019) conducted a trial of 16-week ninety minute group CBT for people with a diagnosis of hoarding disorder and found that saving beliefs change partially mediated outcomes. This was a study with a control. Key components of the group were: in-session practice of discarding, refraining from acquiring, decision-making, problem-solving training, emotional distress tolerance, motivational interviewing strategies, and contingency management.

OTHER THERAPEUTIC MODELS

In an approach like CBT, though slightly different, Ayers et al. (2018) conducted Cognitive Rehabilitation and Exposure/Sorting Therapy (CREST) with Older Adults diagnosed with Hoarding Disorder. This was a randomised controlled trial with participants showing significantly more significant improvement than a case management control group; changes were maintained at six months. CREST involves teaching skills that target prospective memory, planning, cognitive flexibility, and problem-solving, followed by exposure therapy. Ayers et al. (2018) suggest a head-to-head trial between CBT and CREST, and an analysis of the effective components of each.

> *If you set goals, you are setting up potential for failure.*
> Christine

Chou et al. (2020) conducted a pilot study into Compassion-Focused Therapy (CFT) and has had positive outcomes. Again, this is an approach similar to CBT but with enough difference to be considered separately. In the pilot, CFT was used for a second round of treatment for people who had previously received CBT but remained symptomatic. The people who completed a course CFT after the CBT had symptom severity drop below the cut-off point in 77 per cent of cases, whereas those who had a second round was 23 per cent. This was only a pilot, but CFT could be a beneficial adjunct psychological therapy to CBT.

Peer Facilitated Treatment (PFT) has been put forward as an alternative group approach to CBT. This approach involves someone who also has problems with hoarding and facilitating a group working through a manual. Delucchi et al. (2019) randomly allocated 323 adults with a diagnosis of hoarding disorder to a CBT or PFT group. A psychologist led the CBT groups; the PFT groups were led by peers using the manual

> *Will I be giving away part of myself if I give this away?*
>
> Anon

Buried in Treasures (Tolin, Steketee & Frost, 2007). Group PFT was found to be as effective as group CBT. This provides an alternative/complementary approach. It must be noted that the Buried in Treasures approach is based upon a Cognitive Behavioural model. The study demonstrates that if a peer is working from a manual grounded in solid theory, a psychologist is not needed to facilitate the group.

In relation to support groups and intervention groups, treatment orientated support is indicated. However, based upon the evidence, where circumstances allow group CBT for HD should be considered over treatment orientated support groups. More evidence is needed on the severity of the problems in different types of groups in studies going forward. For example, do the people in the support groups have the same level of severity of problem as those in CBT group interventions.

Other approaches have been applied to hoarding problems with different levels of success. Acceptance and commitment therapy (ACT) has been trialled by Kraft (2023) through a web based self-help programme. This was found to be superior to a control, but not as effective as individual CBT. It would be interesting to see like for like with individual therapist delivered ACT trialled against a control. Kraft proposes that ACT has components, such as work on cognitive flexibility that could be beneficial. Cognitive Analytic Therapy (CAT) was not found to be effective in a hermeneutic single-case efficacy design (HSCED) evaluation by Spence et al. (2019). However, this was a study with someone who had also not responded to two previous interventions of CBT.

Given the importance clinically of involving carers, family members and/or agencies supporting the person (e.g. housing associations) evidence is needed on the outcomes of offering a systemic intervention, or Family involvement in therapy, and the most effective way of supporting people to make change.

Challenges

Because hoarding is a relatively newly identified, distinct difficulty within mental health, there are many gaps in our understanding of it and the interventions that may be of use. The challenge for practitioner psychologists as scientist-practitioners is to consider a range of unanswered questions, the most pressing of these major challenges being:

> *Someone coming into your home can feel invasive.*
>
> John

- What are the most acceptable forms of therapy for people who have difficulties with hoarding so as to improve engagement and reduce drop out?
- What interventions for hoarding difficulties are efficacious?
- Are outcomes maintained over time? What is the durability of psychological interventions over the long term?
- To identify the optimal means of service delivery and test whether stepped care models of intervention can be applied according to hoarding severity.

- To compare group and individual interventions within models and build the evidence base for each approach.
- To identify active ingredients of therapy and to continue to test whether home visits add value.
- To identify how aging interacts with hoarding outcomes.
- To identify the differences in experiences between carers who live with the person who hoards and those living away from the home.
- To identify effective interventions that involve families and carers.
- To develop a hoarding-specific therapy competency assessment tool for individual and group CBT.

The often very challenging nature of working with people with hoarding difficulties for practitioner psychologists will be shared across housing support staff, social care staff, environmental health officers and staff from primary care (Tolin et al., 2012). All these staff require access to a psychologically informed understanding of the person who hoards, based on good research evidence and diligent psychosocial assessment. There is a potential role for shared team formulations of clients that hoard, to facilitate the development of a shared language of care and encourage coherence of the team. Practitioner psychologists and psychological professionals have a key role to play in this, and can work to increase empathy among all staff groups.

Practitioner psychology competencies in staff supervision and consultation can be used to support both mental health colleagues and non-mental-health workers. Support staff can benefit from the opportunity to discuss how best to offer practical support in clearing or decluttering.

There is a clear role for practitioner psychologists in offering access to psychological knowledge about the change process and specific difficulties people who hoard face, such as information-processing difficulties. Practitioner psychologists are in a good position to contribute to profession specific advice (e.g. National Housing Federation, 2016), or provide training to others, both in statutory services, voluntary sector and for people who hoard and their carers.

Research

As scientist-practitioners, practitioner psychologists are well placed to contribute to the growing evidence base about hoarding.

Who is the outcome for? The hoarder or the family member?

Anon

The research questions are broader than simply which intervention works best, and centres on the need to consider improving our theoretical understanding of hoarding. The paucity of evidence on effective interventions is nevertheless an ongoing concern. Hoarding is a serious community health problem with significant costs and risks for both the person and their family, their neighbourhood and statutory services. Research that considers the impact of intervening within the wider system as opposed to simply individually, and pays attention to the broader social and psychological consequences, would be welcome. The area offers opportunities for research that goes across disciplines.

Governance

It is important for practitioner psychologists working in this area to have a positive and proactive approach to good clinical governance to maintain quality, to manage risk and to drive improvement. It is best practice to keep the client at the centre of the care. People with hoarding problems may present situations where organisations may see solutions that seem sensible, but not in accordance with the client's wishes. Understanding how to assess capacity and knowing the associated principles help guide clinicians in their decision making in a way that keeps the client at the centre.

> *The lack of awareness some professionals have on the problems and issues hoarders face and the lack of understanding of what a hoarder actually means is frustrating; the lack of empathy... is distressing*
> A carer

Practitioner psychologists working with people who have hoarding problems are working in an area that is new and where the evidence base is developing. Clinicians need to stay up to date with the literature as new findings are published which will lead to changes and adaptations in what they deliver. It is important for clinicians to take a researcher-practitioner approach to their work that takes each case as a possibility for new insights.

Governance around safety when working with hoarding involves both considering the safety of the person with the hoarding problem and those working with them because of possible biohazards. In regards of client safety, the relevant safeguarding legislation needs to be complied with.

Clear leadership is needed in multiagency working to provide a service for this client group where the responsibility of delivering different parts of the care is clear, and where the management of different professional opinions is facilitated in a way that does not adversely affect the client.

People who hoard are often known to several agencies who want to communicate with one another for good reasons. However, there still needs to be concordance with good clinical governance in relation to data handling and sharing.

People working with hoarding problems need to have appropriate training from a provider who has experience and competence in this area. There is a need for wider awareness training within different services who encounter people with hoarding problems so that they can recognise and signpost people appropriately.

For good governance, services need to be keeping a record of people who they are working with who have hoarding problems even if that is not the problem that they are working with, to establish the prevalence levels within their caseload and to make a case for service provision.

Supervision

Practitioner psychologists are familiar with the benefits of regular supervision to ensure safe and appropriate practice. There is a need to ensure others working with hoarding can also access high quality supervision. In particular, staff with little or no professional training can benefit from case consultation and formulation to better understand the difficulties the people they are working with face.

> *Try putting yourself in the hoarder's position; how would you like to be helped with a problem of your own?*
> Harry

Continuing professional development and training

The training needs are clear, both within practitioner psychology and also for the wider networks of people involved in working to support people who hoard.

The public will benefit from improved understanding and awareness of what hoarding is and how it presents. The need to provide psychological models of mental health generally extends to and includes the importance of addressing misunderstandings about hoarding. The training needs of those in our communities who support people generally, be it GPs, social care staff, fire-fighters, workers in mental health non-statutory services and de-clutterers, need to be considered. Service Leads need a better understanding of the specific needs and difficulties with engagement for people with hoarding problems. Training also needs to be provided for people providing therapeutic interventions to those with mental health needs, whether in primary or secondary care, in order to improve the outcomes of psychological interventions for this group.

Service design and workforce planning

The specific needs of people who hoard preclude the use of traditional models of mental health, whereby a person visits their GP requesting help, and is referred to a local service providing individual therapy. A more proactive style of engaging is required, involving neighbours, carers and other agencies that have concerns, which will provide a much more thorough assessment and intervention plan (see BPS 2013b for further information about engaging proactively).

The tendency of services to work as gatekeepers and services of 'exclusion' rather than 'inclusion' may cause problems for hard-to-reach groups such as those with hoarding difficulties. It is clear that in order to reduce risks and improve quality of life, this group of people requires services that are well embedded in communities, able to reach out and respond flexibly, and visit people in their own homes.

Practitioner psychologists' core competencies include psychological formulation, skills in individual therapy and the ability to implement models in a flexible, personalised and planned manner (BPS, 2014b). The importance of meta-competencies that allow adaptation of interventions to the needs of the person and being able to manage 'obstacles' to therapy has also been established (Roth & Pilling, 2007). Competencies in CBT need to be broader than simply techniques applied to a problem. Practitioner psychologists are able to work collaboratively, sharing responsibility for change with individuals, their families and outside agencies. Practitioner psychologists need to be able to take into account different responses, concerns and ideas from family members, and engage with the psychosocial context of the person with hoarding difficulties. Respect, empathy, collaboration and attitudes that support recovery are just as fundamental as therapeutic techniques (Roth & Pilling, 2007; BPS, 2000).

Services for people who hoard need to be provided that work across the lifespan and range of severity of problems via stepped care models of service delivery. Services need to address the needs of people with multiple difficulties, including poor physical health and disabilities both physical and intellectual, and who may also be socially excluded and slow to seek help. The commissioning of education and training must also support the development of knowledge and skills required to work with people who hoard.

Practitioner psychologists are well placed to draw on a range of therapeutic modalities, and intervene with families, services providing support and other organisations. Practitioner psychologists are able to offer supervision, consultation, training and advice on service development, alongside evaluation and research to better inform our work (BPS, 2014b).

Hoarding and the media

Hoarding has held an interesting place in the media, as television programmes depicting hoarding behaviour have had a high profile. If hoarding is considered to be a distinct clinical problem, then its prevalence in programmes far outweighs the other, more common mental health conditions. Until hoarding was labelled as a mental health difficulty, it was treated as an unusual activity that some people engage in and which other people were curious about.

Hoarding can be related to people, their properties and what they keep in them, as part of a larger popular television narrative of property renovations. There are also programmes which touch on aspects of hoarding behaviour concerning the items people keep and the value that they might possess.

Media interest in hoarding is of mixed value. On the one hand, shedding light on the issue may assist in broader understanding. On the other hand, heavily edited coverage may not give the full picture of the complexities and difficulties around hoarding behaviours (Rego, 2011).

Programmes that depict hoarding, such as the USA programme 'Hoarders', may increase public awareness of hoarding, but does this increase people's levels of understanding and compassion or their levels of stigma? An experimental study with student participants by Bates et al. (2020) suggested that people were more stigmatising about hoarding directly after watching a television show containing hoarding depictions. This leads to the question of whether the problem could be depicted in a different way, with a different narrative that leads to more understanding and compassion rather than stigma.

Advice on media representation is available from the British Psychological Society (BPS), and practitioner psychologists are well positioned to provide a psychological view of mental health, wellbeing, and psychological interventions and research. How mental health is represented in the media is in itself an area for debate (Whomsley, 2013) with significant ethical issues to be considered, and improved care for participants now seen as essential. The British Psychological Society has engaged with a range of journalists and regulators to improve the systems in place to protect the public. Guidance has been published (BPS, 2019), media training is available for practitioner psychologists and support given to producers and journalists wanting to identify specific professionals with expertise and a willingness to engage with them.

They go in and clear... What happens in a few months' time? ... I've exposed myself to the nation.
Christine

It's exploitation... both sets have their needs... you're churning people's emotions.
Harry

Before the programmes. I didn't realise there was help out there. It would have helped me to have this information years ago.
Anon

It was only when the programmes were on television that I thought it's actually a mental health problem. Before that I just thought I'm creating clutter.
Anon

Conclusions

Hoarding has attracted increased attention from mental health professionals, social services, the fire service, housing officers and environmental health. It is a problem that can impact on a person's physical and mental health and exacerbate other problems. It is a problem that can lead to social isolation and loneliness. The prevalence rate of hoarding together with the impact on other services and the community merits a specialist service, which would probably be psychologically led.

> *The habit has been controlling us. Now we have to control the habit.*
> Danielle

The existing evidence base suggests that CBT based interventions, individually or in groups, are the most effective psychological intervention. However ideas from other approaches could well augment what is offered. More research is needed to build the evidence base and develop and trial new interventions.

Practitioner psychologists are well placed to take a leading role in this area, not only in delivering interventions but also in advising other staff, policy-makers and the media. Service provision needs to develop to improve engagement and reduce the impairment and distress experienced. The development of multiagency hoarding frameworks has been a welcome development for more organised and coherent working. Mental health and social care services have responsibilities to provide a service for people with hoarding difficulties. Social care have become more involved, possibly as a consequence of the Care Act (2014), whereas Mental Health workers are still sometimes reluctant to be involved.

It is recommended that in working with individuals with hoarding difficulties, interventions need to be behaviourally defined, realistic and achievable, or the work can be overwhelming. However, interventions need to be broader than individually focused, and should address the needs of carers, services and the wider community.

Those working with people with hoarding difficulties should have access to advice, and training, to ensure they have the competencies required for their role and the interventions they are delivering.

It is hoped that this set of good practice guidelines will encourage practitioner psychologists across the UK to take a leading role in improving society's response to hoarding and the difficulties faced by those who hoard.

There is hope for change.

References

Adults with Incapacity (Scotland) Act (2000). Available at: http://www.legislation.gov.uk/asp/2000/4/contents.

Ainsworth, M.D.S., Blehar, M., Waters E., Wall, S. (1978). *Patterns of attachment: A psychological study of the strange situation*. Hillsdale, NJ: Erlbaum.

American Psychiatric Association (2013). *Diagnostic and statistical manual of mental disorders (5th edn)*. Arlington, VA: American Psychiatric Publishing NEED.

Ayers, C.R., Iqbal, Y. & Strickland, K. (2014). Medical conditions in geriatric hoarding disorder patients. *Aging and Mental Health, 18*, 148–151.

Ayers, C.R., Wetherell, J.W., Golshan, S. & Saxena, S. (2011). Cognitive-behavioral therapy for geriatric compulsive hoarding. *Behavior Research and Therapy, 49*, 689–694.

Ayers, C., Dozier, M., Twamley, E., Saxena, S., Granholm, E., Mayes, T. & Wetherell, J. (2018). Cognitive Rehabilitation and Exposure/Sorting Therapy (CREST) for Hoarding Disorder in older adults: A randomized clinical trial. *The Journal of Clinical Psychiatry, 79*(2), 85–93. http://dx.doi.org/10.4088/jcp.16m11072 Retrieved from https://escholarship.org/uc/item/6jj629vx

Baker, S.M. & Gentry, J.W. (1996). Kids as collectors: A phenomenological study of first and fifth graders. *Advances in Consumer Research, 23*, 132–137.

Baron-Cohen, S. (1989) Do autistic children have obsessions and compulsions? *British Journal of Clinical Psychology, 28*(3), 193–200.

Bates,S.,De Leonardis, A.J.,Corrigan, P.W. & Chasson, G.S. (2020). Buried in stigma: Experimental investigation of the impact of hoarding depictions in reality television on public perception. *Journal of Obsessive-Compulsive and Related Disorders, 26*, 2020,100538. https://doi.org/10.1016/j.jocrd.2020.100538.

Bloch, M.H., Landeros-Weisenberger, A., Rosario, M.C., Pittenger, C. & Leckman, J.F. (2008). Meta-analysis of the symptom structure of obsessive-compulsive disorder. *American Journal of Psychiatry, 165*, 1532–1542.

Bodryzlova, Y., Audet , J.S., Bergeron, K. & O'Connor, K. (2019). Group cognitive-behavioural therapy for hoarding disorder: Systematic review and meta-analysis. *Health Soc Care Community. 2019 May;27*(3):517–530. doi:10.1111/hsc.12598. Epub 2018 Jul 23. PMID: 30033635.

Bowlby, J. (1969/82). *Attachment and loss: Vol 1. Attachment*. 2nd. New York: Basic Books.

Bratiotis, C., Woody, S. & Lauster, N. (2019). Coordinated community-based hoarding interventions: Evidence of case management practices. *Families in Society, 100*(1), 93–105. https://doi.org/10.1177/1044389418802450

Bream, V. (2013, July). A new formulation for hoarding – Introducing the vicious shamrock. Paper presented at the annual conference of the British Association for Behavioural and Cognitive Psychotherapies, London.

British Psychological Society (2000). *Recent advances in understanding mental illness and psychotic experiences.* Leicester: Author.

British Psychological Society (2005). *Discussion paper: DCP policy on continued supervision.* Leicester: Author.

British Psychological Society (2006). *Assessment of capacity in adults: Interim guidance for psychologists.* Leicester: Author.

British Psychological Society (2011). *Good practice guidelines on the use of psychological formulation.* Leicester: Author.

British Psychological Society (2013a). *Classification of behaviour and experience in relation to functional psychiatric diagnoses: time for a paradigm shift.* Leicester: Author.

British Psychological Society (2013b). *Clinical psychologists and assertive outreach briefing paper No. 21.* Leicester: Author.

British Psychological Society (2014b). *National mental health, well-being and psychological therapies – the role of clinical psychology. A briefing paper for NHS commissioners.* Leicester: Author.

British Psychological Society (2014a). *Safeguarding and promoting the welfare of children: A position paper.* Leicester: Author.

British Psychological Society (2019). *BPS Guidance: 'What makes a good assessment of capacity'* https://explore.bps.org.uk/content/report-guideline/bpsrep.2019.rep127

British Psychological Society (2019). *Psychology and Media Productions: Guidance for commissioners and producers.* Leicester: Author.

Burton, C.L., Arnold, P.D. & Soreni, N. (2015). Three reasons why studying hoarding in children and adolescents is important. *J Can Acad Child Adolesc Psychiatry. 2015 Fall;24*(2), 128–30. Epub 2015 Aug 31. PMID: 26379725; PMCID: PMC4558984.

Busch, A. (2004). *The uncommon life of common objects.* New York: Metropolis Books.

Büscher, T.P., Dyson, J. & Cowdell, F. (2013). The effects of hoarding disorder on families: an integrative review. *Journal of Psychiatric and Mental Health Nursing.* doi:10.1111/jpm.12098.

Cermele, J.A., Melendez-Pallitto, L. & Pandina, G.J. (2001). Intervention in compulsive hoarding. A case study. *Behavior Modification, 25*, 214–232.

Chaplin, L.N. & John, D.R. (2007). Growing up in a material world: Age differences in materialism in children and adolescents. *Journal of Consumer Research, 34*(4), 480–493.

Chasson, G., Carpenter, A., Ewing, J., Gibby, B. & Lee, N. (2014). Empowering families to help a loved one with hoarding disorder: Pilot study of family-as-motivators training. *Behaviour Research and Therapy, 63*, 9–16.

Chia, K., Pasalich, D.S., Fassnacht, D.B., Ali, K., Kyrios, M., Maclean, B. & Grisham, J.R. (2021). Interpersonal attachment, early family environment, and trauma in hoarding: A systematic review. *Clinical Psychology Review, 90*, 102096.

Chou, C.Y., Tsoh, J.Y., Shumway, M., Smith, L.C., Chan, J., Delucchi, K., Tirch, D., Gilbert, P. & Mathews, C.A. (2020). Treating hoarding disorder with compassion-focused therapy: A pilot study examining treatment feasibility, acceptability, and exploring treatment effects. *Br J Clin Psychol. 2020 Mar;59*(1):1–21. doi:10.1111/bjc.12228. Epub 2019 Jul 4. PMID: 31271462.

Clarke, D.J., Boer, H., Whittington, J., Holland, A., Butler, J. & Webb, T. (2002). Prader-Willi Syndrome, compulsive and ritualistic behaviour: The first population-based survey. *British Journal of Psychiatry, 180*, 358–362.

Cromer, K.R., Schmidt, N.B. & Murphy, D.L. (2007). Do traumatic events influence the clinical expression of compulsive hoarding? *Behaviour Research and Therapy, 45*, 2581–2592.

David, J., Crone, C. & Norberg, M.M. (2022). A critical review of cognitive behavioural therapy for hoarding disorder: How can we improve outcomes? *Clinical Psychology & Psychotherapy, 29*(2), 469–488.

Davidson, E,J., Dozier, M.E., Mayes, T.L., Baer, K.A. & Ayers, C.R. (2020). Family and social functioning in adults with hoarding disorder. *Children Australia. 2020;45*(3), 159–163. doi:10.1017/cha.2020.20

DCP Policy on Supervision (BPS, 2014) https://explore.bps.org.uk/content/report-guideline/bpsrep.2014.inf224

DCP Report on Understanding Psychosis and Schizophrenia (BPS, 2017) https://explore.bps.org.uk/content/report-guideline/bpsrep.2017.rep03

Deary, I.J., Corley, J., Gow, A.J., Harris, S.E., Houlihan, L.M., Marioni, R.E., Penke, L., Rafnsson, S.B. & Starr, J.M. (2009). Age-associated cognitive decline. *British Medical Bulletin, 92*, 135–152.

Delucchi, K.L., Mathews, C.A., Mackin, R.S. et al. (2019). Comparing Peer-Led Support Groups with Therapist-Led Support Groups for Treating Hoarding Disorder [Internet]. Washington (DC): Patient-Centered Outcomes Research Institute (PCORI). Available from: https://www.ncbi.nlm.nih.gov/books/NBK595719/ doi: 10.25302/5.2019.CE.13046000

Department of Education and Skills (2003). *Every child matters: Change for children.* Norwich: The Stationery Office.

Department of Health (2000). *No secrets: Guidance on developing and implementing multi-agency policies and procedures to protect vulnerable adults from abuse.* London: Department of Health.

Department of Health (2014). Care Bill becomes Care Act [Electronic version]. Retrieved 20 June 2014 from https://www.gov.uk/government/speeches/care-bill-becomes-care-act-2014.

Drury, H., Ajmi, S., Fernández de la Cruz, L., Nordsletten, A.E. & Mataix-Cols, D. (2014). Caregiver burden, family accommodation, health, and well-being in relatives of individuals with hoarding disorder. *Journal of Affective Disorders, 159*, 7–14.

Dykens, E.M., Leckman, J.F. & Cassidy, S.B. (1996). Obsessions and compulsions in Prader-Willi Syndrome. *Journal of Child Psychology and Psychiatry and Allied Disciplines, 37*(8), 995–1002.

Eckfield, M.B. & Wallhagen, M.I. (2013).The synergistic effect of growing older with hoarding behaviors. *Clinical Nursing Research, 22*(4), 475–491.

Edwards, V., Salkovskis, P.M. & Bream, V. (2023). Do they really care? Specificity of social support issues in hoarding disorder and obsessive–compulsive disorder. *British Journal of Clinical Psychology, 62,* 573–591. https://doi.org/10.1111/bjc.12426PM

Ehrlich, T. (2012). Why can't I clean up my iphone? Retrieved 28 June 2014 from http://geardiary.com/2012/02/26/hoarding-why-can-i-not-clean-up-my-iphone/.

Fernández de la Cruz, L., E Nordsletten, A. & Mataix-Cols, D. (2016). Ethnocultural aspects of hoarding disorder. *Current Psychiatry Reviews, 12*(2), 115–123.

Frank, H., Stewart, E., Walther, M., Benito, K., Freeman, J., Conelea. C. & Garci, A. (2014). Hoarding behavior among young children with obsessive-compulsive disorder. *Journal of Obsessive-compulsive and Related Disorders, 3*(1), 6–11.

Frost, R.O., Steketee, G. & Williams, L.(2000). Hoarding: a community health problem. *Health and Social Care Community, 8*, 229–34. 10.1046/j.1365-2524.2000.00245.x

Frost, R.O., Steketee, G., Tolin, D.F. & Renaud, S. (2008). Development and validation of the clutter image rating scale. *Journal of Personality and Behavioural Assessment, 30*, 193–203.

Frost, R.O., Steketee, G. & Tolin, D.F. (2011a). Comorbidity in hoarding disorder. *Depression and Anxiety, 28*(10), 876–884.

Frost, R., Tolin, D., Steketee, G. & Oh, M. (2011b). Indecisiveness and hoarding. *International Journal of Cognitive Therapy, 4*(3), 253–262.

Frost, R.O., Pekareva-Kochergina, A. & Maxner, S. (2011c). The effectiveness of a biblio-based support group for hoarding disorder. *Behaviour Research and Therapy, 49*, 628–634.

Frost, R.O., Ruby, D. & Shuer, L.J. (2012). The buried in treasures workshop: Waitlist control trial of facilitated support groups for hoarding. *Behaviour Research and Therapy, 50,* 661–667.

Gilliam, C.M., Norberg, M.M., Villavicencio, A., Morrison, S., Hannan, S.E. & Tolin, D.F. (2011). Group cognitive behavioral therapy for hoarding disorder: An open trial. *Behaviour Research and Therapy, 49,* 802–807.

Girsham, P. (2011). Massive clean up is no cure for hoarding. Retrieved 20 June 2014 from http://www.npr.org/blogs/health/2011/05/02/135919186/-big-clean-out-is-no-cure-for- hoarding.

Gledhill, L.J., Bream, V., Drury, H. & Onwumere, J. (2021). Information processing in hoarding disorder: A systematic review of the evidence. *Journal of Affective Disorders Reports, 3,* 100039. https://doi.org/10.1016/j.jadr.2020.100039

Goodman, W.K., Price, L.H., Rasmussen, S.A., Mazure, C., Fleischmann, R.L., Hill, C.L., Heninger, G.R. & Charney, D.S. (1989). The Yale-Brown Obsessive Compulsive Scale. Development, use, and reliability. *Archives of General Psychiatry, 46*(11), 1006–1011.

Grassi, G., Moradei, C., Cecchelli, C. & van Ameringen, M. (2023). Who really hoards? Hoarding symptoms in adults with attention-deficit hyperactivity disorder (ADHD), obsessive-compulsive disorder (OCD) and healthy controls, *Journal of Psychiatric Research, Volume 166*, 2023, 74–79. https://doi.org/10.1016/j.jpsychires.2023.09.006. (https://www.sciencedirect.com/science/article/pii/S002239562300417X)

Grisham, J.R., Brown, T.A., Liverant, G.I. & Campbell-Sills, L. (2005). The distinctiveness of compulsive hoarding from obsessive-compulsive disorder. *Journal of Anxiety Disorders, 19*, 767–779.

Grisham, J.R., Brown, T.A., Savage, C.R., Steketee, G. & Barlow, D.H. (2007). Neuropsychological impairment associated with compulsive hoarding. *Behaviour Research and Therapy, 45*, 1471–1483.

Grisham, J.R., Norberg, M.M., Williams, A.D., Certoma, S.P. & Kadib, R. (2010). Categorization and cognitive deficits in compulsive hoarding. *Behaviour Research and Therapy, 48*, 866–872.

Hacker, L.E., Park, J.M., Timpano, K.R., Cavitt, M.A., Alvaro, J.L., Lewin, A.B., Murphy, T.K. & Storch, E.A. (2012). Hoarding in children with ADHD. *Journal of Attention Disorders*. e-pub. doi: 10.1177/1087054712455845.

Haighton, C., Caiazza, R., Neave, N. (2023). "In an ideal world that would be a multiagency service because you need everybody's expertise." Managing hoarding disorder: A qualitative investigation of existing procedures and practices. *PLoS One. 2023 Mar 9;18*(3):e0282365. doi: 10.1371/journal.pone.0282365. PMID: 36893136; PMCID: PMC9997939.

Hartl, T. & Frost, R.O. (1999). Cognitive-behavioral treatment of compulsive hoarding: a multiple baseline experimental case study. *Behaviour Research and Therapy, 37*(5), 451–461.

Hartl, T.L., Duffany, S., Allen, G.J., Steketee, G. & Frost, R.O. (2005). Relationships among compulsive hoarding, trauma, and attention-deficit/hyperactivity disorder. *Behaviour Research and Therapy, 43*(2), 269–276.

Hartl, T.L., Frost, R.O., Allen, G.J., Deckersbach, T., Steketee, G. & Duffany, S.R. (2004). Actual and perceived memory deficits in individuals with compulsive hoarding. *Depression and Anxiety, 20*, 59–69.

Health and Care Professions Council (2007). Equality and diversity scheme [Electronic version]. Retrieved 4 july 2014 from http://www.hcpc-uk.org/assets/documents/ 100021B1HPCEqualityandDiversityScheme.pdf.

Hill K., Yates, D., Dean, R. & Stavisky. J. (2019).A novel approach to welfare interventions in problem multi-cat households. *BMC Vet Res. 2019 Dec 3;15*(1):434. doi:10.1186/s12917-019-2183-3. PMID: 31796018; PMCID: PMC6891977.

Hoarding of Animals Resource Consortium (2013). Retrieved 10 November from http://www.tufts.edu/vet/ hoarding/index.html.

Holmes, S., Wolter, P. & Harris, C. (2014). Developing a self-help group for people with hoarding disorder and their carers. *Mental Health Today, Sep/Oct 24–27.*

Holroyd, S. & Price, H. (2009). Hoarding and how to approach it. Unpublished guidance for environmental health officers. Chartered Institute of Environmental Health.

Hwang, J.-P., Tsai, S.-J., Yang, C.-H., Liu, K.-M. & Ling, J.F. (1998). Hoarding behavior in dementia: A preliminary report. *American Journal of Geriatric Psychiatry, 6*(4), 285–289.

Iervolino, A.C., Perroud,N., Fullana, M.A., Guipponi, M., Cherkas, L. & Collier, D.A. (2009). Prevalence and heritability of compulsive hoarding: A twin study. *American Journal of Psychiatry, 166*, 1156–1161.

International Classification of Diseases, Eleventh Revision (ICD-11), World Health Organization (WHO) 2019/2021 https:// icd.who.int/browse11.

Jacobson, N.S. & Truax, P. (1991). Clinical significance: A statistical approach to defining meaningful change in psychotherapy research. *Journal of Consulting and Clinical Psychology. 59.* 12–19.

Jarrett, C. (2013). The psychology of stuff and things. *The Psychologist, 26*(8), 560–565.

Kellett, S. (2007). Compulsive hoarding: A site-security model and associated psychological treatment strategies. *Clinical Psychology and Psychotherapy, 14*(6), 413–427.

Kellett, S., Greenhalgh, R., Beail, N. & Ridgway, N. (2010). Compulsive hoarding: An interpretative phenomenological analysis. *Behavioural & Cognitive Psychotherapy, 38*, 141–156.

Kellett, S. & Holden, K. (2014). Emotional attachment to objects in hoarding: A critical review of the evidence. In R.A. Frost & G. Steketee (Eds.) *The Oxford handbook of hoarding and acquiring.* Oxford: OUP.

Kellett, S., Matuozzo, H. & Kotecha, C. (2015). Effectiveness of cognitive-behaviour therapy for hoarding disorder in people with mild intellectual disabilities. *Research in Developmental Disabilities, 47,* 385–392.

Knight, B.G. (1999). Scientific bias for psychotherapeutic interventions with older adults: An overview. *Journal of Clinical Psychology, 55,* 927–934.

Krafft, J., Petersen, J.M., Ong, C.W., Twohig, M.P. & Levin, M.E. (2023). Making space: A randomized waitlist-controlled trial of an acceptance and commitment therapy website for hoarding. *Journal of Obsessive-Compulsive and Related Disorders, 39,* 100846. (And there are other studies).

Laidlaw, K., Thompson, L.W., Gallagher-Thompson, D. & Dick-Siskin, L. (2003). *Cognitive behaviour therapy with older people.* Chichester: John Wiley & Sons.

Landau, D., Iervolinoa, A.C., Pertusa, A., Santoa, S., Singh, S. & Mataix-Cols, D. (2011). Stressful life events and material deprivation in hoarding disorder. *Journal of Anxiety Disorders, 25*(2), 192–202.

Levy, H.C., Worden, B.L., Gilliam, C.M., D'Urso, C., Steketee, G., Frost, R.O. & Tolin, D.F. (2017). Changes in saving cognitions mediate hoarding symptom change in cognitive-behavioral therapy for hoarding disorder. *Journal of Obsessive-compulsive and Related Disorders, 14,* 112–118.

London Fire Brigade (2023). Firefighters offer support to those with hoarding tendencies over concerns cost of living crisis could increase fire risk. https://www.london-fire.gov.uk/news/2023/may/firefighters-offer-support-to-those-with-hoarding-tendencies-over-concerns-cost-of-living-crisis-could-increase-fire-risk/

Mackin, R.S., Arean, P.A., Delucchi, K.L. & Mathews, C.A. (2011). Cognitive functioning in individuals with severe compulsive hoarding behaviors and late life depression. *International Journal of Geriatric Psychiatry, 26,* 314–321.

Mataix-Cols, D., Frost, R.O., Pertusa, M.D., Clark, L.A., Saxena, S., Leckman, J.F., Stein, D.J., Matsunaga, H. & Wilhelm, S. (2010). Hoarding disorder: A new diagnosis for DSM-V. *International Journal of Geriatric Psychiatry, 27*(6), 556–572.

Mataix-Cols, D. & Fernández de la Cruz, L. (2018). Hoarding disorder has finally arrived, but many challenges lie ahead. *World Psychiatry, 17*(2), 224–225. First published: 24 May 2018. https://doi.org/10.1002/wps.20531

Mathes, B.M., Timpano, K.R., Raines, A.M. & Schmidt, N.B. (2020). Attachment theory and hoarding disorder: A review and theoretical integration. *Behaviour Research and Therapy, 125,* 103549.

McGrath, M., Russell, A.M. & Masterson, C. (2024). 'A more human approach… I haven't found that really': experiences of hoarding difficulties and seeking help. *Behavioural and Cognitive Psychotherapy, 52*(1), 1–13.

McKellar, K., Sillence, E., Neave, N. & Briggs, P. (2020). There is more than one type of hoarder: Collecting, managing and hoarding digital data in the workplace. *Interacting with Computers, 32*(3), 209–220. https://doi.org/10.1093/iwc/iwaa015

McMillan, S.G., Rees, C.S. & Pestell, C. (2013). An investigation of executive functioning, attention and working memory in compulsive hoarding. *Behavioral and Cognitive Psychotherapy, 41*(5), 610–625.

Medard, E. & Kellett, S. (2014). The role of adult attachment and social support in hoarding disorder. *Behavioral and Cognitive Psychotherapy, 42*(5), 629–633.

Midlands Psychology Group (2014). The draft manifesto. *Clinical Psychology Forum, 256,* 3–7.

Miller, W.R. & Rollnick, S. (2013). *Motivational interviewing: Helping people change (3rd edn)*. New York: Guilford.

Moran, D. & Patterson, J.L. (2011). *Animal hoarding: A pervasive problem*. Retrieved 25 June 2014 from http://www.psychologytoday.com/blog/when-more-isnt-enough/201109/animal- hoarding-pervasive-problem.

Morein-Zamir, S., Kasese, M., Chamberlain, S.R. & Trachtenberg, E. (2021). Elevated levels of hoarding in ADHD: A special link with inattention. *J Psychiatr Res. 2021 Dec 13;145,* 167–174. doi:10.1016/j.jpsychires.2021.12.024. Epub ahead of print. PMID: 34923357; PMCID: PMC7612156.

Mueller, A., Mitchell, J.E., Crosby, R.D., Glaesmer, H. & de Zwaan, M. (2009). The prevalence of compulsive hoarding and its association with compulsive buying in a German population- based sample. *Behaviour Research and Therapy, 47,* 705–709.

Muroff, J., Steketee, G., Rasmussen, J., Gibson, A., Bratiotis, C. & Sorrentino, C.M. (2009). Group cognitive and behavioral treatment for compulsive hoarding. *Depression and Anxiety, 26,* 634–640.

Muroff, J., Bratitiotis, C. & Steketee, G. (2011). Treatment for hoarding behaviors: A review of the evidence. *Clinical Social Work Journal, 39,* 406–423.

Muroff, J., Steketee, G., Himle, J. & Frost, R. (2010). Delivery of internet treatment for compulsive hoarding (D.I.T.C.H.). *Behaviour Research and Therapy, 48,* 79–85.

Muroff, J., Steketee, G., Bratiotis, C. & Ross, A. (2012). Group cognitive and behavioral therapy and bibliotherapy for hoarding: A pilot trial. *Depression and Anxiety, 29*(7), 597–604. doi:10.1002/da.21923.

Nathanson, J.N. & Patronek, G.J. (2011). 'Animal Hoarding: How the Semblance of a Benevolent Mission Becomes Actualized as Egoism and Cruelty'. In Barbara Oakley and others (Eds.) *Pathological Altruism (2011; online edn, Oxford Academic, 19 Jan. 2012)*. https://doi.org/10.1093/acprof:oso/9780199738571.003.0085, accessed 28 February 2024.

National Health Service (2014). Compulsive hoarding: NHS choices [Electronic version]. Retrieved 20 June 2014 from http://www.nhs.uk/Conditions/hoarding/Pages/introduction.aspx.

National Housing Federation (2016). Hoarding: Key considerations and examples of best practice.

National Institute for Health and Clinical Excellence (2005). *Obsessive-compulsive disorder. Clinical Guideline 31.* London: NICE.

Neave, N., Caiazza, R., Hamilton, C., McInnes, L., Saxton, T. K., Deary, V. & Wood, M. (2017). The economic costs of hoarding behaviours in local authority / housing association tenants and private home owners in the north east of England. *Public Health, 148,* 137–139. doi:http://dx.doi.org/10.1016/j.puhe.2017.04.010

Norberg, M.M, Chasson, G.S. & Tolin, D.F. (2021). A standardized approach to calculating clinically significant change in Hoarding Disorder using the Saving Inventory-Revised. *Journal of Obsessive Compulsive and Related Disorders, 28*:100609. doi:10.1016/j.jocrd.2020.100609.

Nordsletten, A.E., Fernández de la Cruz, L., Billotti, D. & Mataix-Cols, D. (2013a). Finders keepers: The features differentiating hoarding disorder from normative collecting. *Comprehensive Psychiatry, 54,* 229–237.

Nordsletten, A.E., Fernandez de la Cruz, L., Pertusa, A., Reichenberg, A., Hatch, S.L. & Mataix-Cols, D. (2013b). The structured interview for hoarding disorder (SIHD): Development, usage and further validation. *Journal of Obsessive Compulsive and Related Disorders, 2*(3), 346–350.

Nordsletten, A.E., Fernández de la Cruz, L., Drury, H., Ajmi, S., Saleem, S. & Mataix-Cols, D. (2014). The family impact scale for hoarding (FISH): Measure development and initial validation. *Journal of Obsessive-compulsive and Related Disorders, 3*(1), 29–34.

Nordsletten, A.E. & Mataix-Cols, D. (2012). Hoarding versus collecting: where does pathology diverge from play? *Clinical Psychology Review, 32*(3), 165–176.

Nordsletten, A.E., Fernandez de la Cruz, L., Aluco, E., Alonso, P., López-Solà, C., Menchón, J.M., Nakao, T., Kuwano, M., Yamada, S., Fontenelle, L.F., Campos- Lima, A.L. & Mataix-Cols, D. (2018). A transcultural study of hoarding disorder:52 Insights from the United Kingdom, Spain, Japan, and Brazil. *Transcultural Psychiatry, 55*(2), 261–285.

Norton, M., Kellett, S., Huddy, V. & Simmonds-Buckley, M. (2024). Household factors and prevalence of squalor: meta-analysis and meta-regression. *BMC Public Health. 5;24*(1), 479. doi:10.1186/s12889-024-17983-3.

Novack, M. (2010). Rooms of shame: Senior move managers' perspective on hoarding. *Journal of Geriatric Care Management, 2,* 21–24.

Nutley, S.K., Camacho, M.R., Eichenbaum, J., Nosheny, R.L., Weiner, M., Delucchi, K.L., Mackin, R.S. & Mathews, C.A. (2021). Hoarding disorder is associated with self-reported cardiovascular / metabolic dysfunction, chronic pain, and sleep apnea. *Journal of Psychiatric Research, Volume 134, 2021,* 15–21. https://doi.org/10.1016/j.jpsychires.2020.12.032.

Nutley, S.K., Read, M., Martinez, S., Eichenbaum, J., Nosheny, R.L., Weiner, M., Mackin, R.S. & Mathews, C.A. (2022). Hoarding symptoms are associated with higher rates of disability than other medical and psychiatric disorders across multiple domains of functioning. *BMC Psychiatry. 2022 Oct 15;22*(1), 647. doi:10.1186/s12888-022-04287-2. PMID: 36241971; PMCID: PMC9569124.

Pearce, S.M. (1998). *Collecting in contemporary practice*. London: Sage Publications.

Pekareva-Kochergina, A. & Frost, R.O. (2009, July). The effects of a biblio-based self-help program for compulsive hoarding. Paper presented at the annual conference of the British Association of Behavioural and Cognitive Psychotherapies, Exeter.

Pertusa, A., Bejerot, S., Eriksson, J., Fernandez de la Cruz, L., Bonde, S., Russell, A. & Mataix-Cols, D. (2012). Do patients with hoarding disorder have autistic traits? *Depression and Anxiety, 29*, 210–218.

Pertusa, A., Frost, R.O. & Mataix-Cols, D. (2010). When hoarding is a symptom of OCD: A case series and implications for DSM-V. *Behaviour Research and Therapy, 48*, 1012–1020.

Pertusa, A., Fullana, M.A., Singh, S., Alonso, P., Menchon, J.M. & Mataix-Cols, D. (2008). Compulsive hoarding: OCD symptom, distinct clinical syndrome, or both. *American Journal of Psychiatry, 165*(10), 1289–1298.

Plimpton, E.H., Frost, R.O., Abbey, B.C. & Dorer, W. (2009). Compulsive hoarding in children: Six case studies. *International Journal of Cognitive Therapy, 2*(1), 88–104.

Pollock, L., Kellett, S. & Totterdell, P. (2014). An intensive time-series evaluation of the effectiveness of cognitive behaviour thera-py for hoarding disorder: A 2-year prospective study. *Psychotherapy Research, 24*(4), 485–495.

Postlethwaite A., Kellett, S. & Mataix-Cols, D. (2019). Prevalence of Hoarding Disorder: A systematic review and meta-analysis. *J Affect Disord. 2019 Sep 1;256*, 309–316. doi:10.1016/j.jad.2019.06.004. Epub 2019 Jun 4. PMID: 31200169.

Prato-Previde, E., Basso Ricci, E. & Colombo, E.S. (2022). The Complexity of the Human-Animal Bond: Empathy, Attachment and Anthropomorphism in Human-Animal Relationships and Animal Hoarding. *Animals (Basel). 2022 Oct 19;12*(20), 2835. doi:10.3390/ani12202835. PMID: 36290219; PMCID: PMC9597799.

Prochaska, J. & DiClemente, C. (1983). Stages and processes of self-change in smoking: toward an integrative model of change. *Journal of Consulting and Clinical Psychology, 5*, 390–395.

Proctor, C, & Rahman, S. (2022). The etiopathogenesis of Diogenes Syndrome. *International Journal of Psychiatry, 7*(1),10–3.

Rees, C.S., Valentine, V. & Anderson, R.A. (2018). The impact of parental hoarding on the lives of children: Interviews with adult offspring of parents with hoarding disorder. *Clinical Psychologist, 22*(3), 327–335. doi:10.1111/cp.12135

Rego, S. (2011). The rise of hoarding. BBC News Magazine [Electronic version]. Retrieved 10 November 2013 from http://www.bbc.co.uk/news/magazine-16299670.

Reinisch, A.I. (2008). Understanding the human aspects of animal hoarding [Electronic version]. *Canadian Veterinary Journal, 49*(12), 1211–1214.

Rodgers, N., McDonald, S. & Wootton, B.M. (2021). Cognitive behavioral therapy for hoarding disorder: An updated meta-analysis. *Journal of Affective Disorders, 290*, 128–135.

Rossiter, R. & Holmes, S. (2013). Access all areas: creative adaptations for CBT with people with cognitive impairments – illustrations and issues [Electronic version]. *Cognitive Behaviour Therapist, 6, e9*, 1–16.

Roth, A. & Pilling, S. (2007). *The competencies required to deliver effective cognitive and behavioural therapy for people with depression and with anxiety disorders.* London: Department of Health.

Sampson, J.M. (2013). The lived experience of family members of persons who compulsively hoard: A qualitative study. *Journal of Marital and Family Therapy, 39*(3), 388–402.

Sampson, J.M., Yeats, J.R. & Harris, S.M. (2012). An evaluation of an ambiguous loss based psychoeducational support group for family members of persons who hoard: A pilot study. *Contemporary Family Therapy: An International Journal, 34*(4), 566–581.

Samuels, J.F., Bienvenu, J.O., Grados, M.O, Cullen, B., Riddle, M.A., Liang, K.Y., Eaton, W.W. & Nestadt,

G. (2008). Prevalence and correlates of hoarding behavior in a community-based sample. *Behaviour Research and Therapy, 46*(7), 836–844.

Samuels, J.F., Bienvenu, O.J., Pinto, A., Fyer, A.J., McCracken, J.T., Rauch, S.L., Murphy, D.L., Grados, M.A., Greenberg, B.D., Knowles, J.A., Piacentini, J., Cannistraro, P.A., Cullen, B. & Riddle, M.A. (2007). Hoarding in obsessive-compulsive disorder: Results from the OCD collaborative genetics study. *Behaviour Research and Therapy, 45*(4), 673–686.

Samuels, J., Bienvenu, O.J., Riddle, M.A., Cullen, B.A., Grados, M.A., Liang, K.Y., Hoehn-Saric, R. & Nestadt, G. (2002). Hoarding in obsessive compulsive disorder: results from a case-control study. *Behaviour Research and Therapy, 40*(5), 517–528.

Shafran, R. & Tallis, F. (1996). Obsessive-compulsive hoarding: A cognitive-behavioural approach. *Behavioural and Cognitive Psychotherapy, 24*, 209–221.

Skirrow, P., Jackson, P.G., Perry, E.P. & Hare, D.J. (2014). I collect therefore I am: The role of 'autonoetic' consciousness and hoarding in Asperger syndrome [Electronic version]. *Clinical Psychology & Psychotherapy.* doi:10.1002/cpp.1889.

Snowdon, J., Shah, A. & Halliday, G. (2007). Severe domestic squalor: a review. *International Psychogeriatrics, 19*, 37–51. 10.1017/S1041610206004236

Snowdon, J., Halliday, G. & Banerjee, S. (2012). *Severe domestic squalor.* Cambridge: Cambridge University Press.

South, M., Ozonoff, S. & McMahon, W.M. (2005). Repetitive behavior profiles in Asperger syndrome and high-functioning autism. *Journal of Autism and Developmental Disorders, 35*, 145–148.

Spence, C., Kellett, S., Totterdell, P. & Parry, G. (2019). Can cognitive analytic therapy treat hoarding disorder? An adjudicated hermeneutic single-case efficacy design evaluation. *Clinical Psychology & Psychotherapy, 26*(6), 673–683.

Steketee, G. (1993). Social support and treatment outcome of obsessive compulsive disorder at 9-month follow-up. *Behavioural and Cognitive Psychotherapy, 21*(2), 81–95.

Steketee, G. & Frost, R. (2003). Compulsive hoarding: Current status of the research. *Clinical Psychology Review, 23*, 905–927.

Steketee, G. & Frost, R.O. (2007). *Compulsive hoarding and acquiring: Therapist guide.* New York: Oxford University Press.

Steketee, G. & Frost, R. (2014a). *Treatment for hoarding disorder therapist guide (2nd edn).* New York: Oxford University Press.

Steketee, G. & Frost, R. (2014b). *Treatment for hoarding disorder workbook (2nd edn).* New York: Oxford University Press.

Steketee, G., Frost, R.O., Tolin, D.F., Rasmussen, J. & Brown, T.A. (2010). Waitlist-controlled trial of cognitive behavior therapy for hoarding disorder. *Depression and Anxiety, 27*(5), 476–484.

Steketee, G., Frost, R., Wincze, J., A., Greene, K. & Douglas, H. (2000). Group and individual treatment of compulsive hoarding: A pilot study. *Behavior and Cognitive Psychotherapy, 28*, 259–268.

Storch, E.A., Muroff, J., Lewin, A.B., Geller, D., Ross, A., McCarthy, K., Morgan, J., Murphy, T.K., Frost, R. & Steketee, G. (2011b). Development and preliminary psychometric evaluation of the Children's Saving Inventory. *Child Psychiatry and Human Development, 42*(2), 166–82.

Storch, E.A, Rahman, O., Park, J.M., Reid, J., Murphy, T.K. & Lewin, A.B. (2011a). Compulsive hoarding in children. *Journal of Clinical Psychology, 67*(5), 507–516.

Stumpf, B.P., De Souza, L.C., Mourão, M.S., Rocha, F.L., Fontenelle, L.F. & Barbosa, I.G. (2023). Cognitive impairment in hoarding disorder: a systematic review. *CNS spectrums, 28*(3), 300–312.

Subkowski, P. (2006). On the psychodynamics of collecting. *International Journal of Psychoanalysis, 87,* 383–401.

Sweeten, G., Sillence, E. & Neave, N. (2018).Digital hoarding behaviours: Underlying motivations and potential negative consequences. *Computers in Human Behavior, 85,* 54–60. https://doi.org/10.1016/j.chb.2018.03.031.

Taylor, J.K., Theiler, S., Nedeljkovic, M. & Moulding, R. (2018). *A qualitative analysis of emotion and emotion regulation in hoarding disorder.* First published: https://doi.org/10.1002/jclp.22715

Testa, R., Pantelis, C. & Fontenelle, L.F. (2011). Hoarding behaviors in children with learning disabilities. *Journal of Child Neurology, 26*(5), 574–579.

The Adult Support and Protection (Scotland) Act (2007) Available at: https://www.legislation.gov.uk/asp/2007/10/contents

Tinlin-Dixon, R. & Stevenson, L. (2022). The 'Northumberland MDT Hoarding Pathway' (N-MDT-HP): Developing a community mental health multidisciplinary team approach to working with individuals with hoarding behaviours. *FPOP Bulletin: Psychology of Older People, 159,* 65–72. 10.53841/bpsfpop.2022.1.159.65.

Tolin, D.F., Fitch, K.E., Frost, R.O. & Steketee, G. (2010). Family informants' perceptions of insight in compulsive hoarding. *Cognitive Therapy and Research, 34*(1) 69–81.

Tolin, D.F., Frost, R.O. & Steketee, G. (2007). An open trial of cognitive-behavioural therapy for compulsive hoarding. *Behaviour Research and Therapy, 45*(7), 1461–1470.

Tolin, D., Frost, R. & Steketee, G. (2012). Working with hoarding vs. non-hoarding clients: A survey of professionals' attitudes and experiences. *Journal of Obsessive-compulsive and Related Disorders, 1*, 48–53.

Tolin, D. Frost, R.O. & Steketee, G. (2014). *Buried in treasures: Help for compulsive hoarding (2nd edn).* New York: Oxford University Press.

Tolin, D.F., Frost, R.O., Steketee, G., Gray, K.D. & Fitch, K.E. (2008a). The economic and social burden of compulsive hoarding. *Psychiatry Research, 160*(2), 200–211.

Tolin, D.F., Frost, R.O., Steketee, G. & Fitch, K.E. (2008b). Family burden of compulsive hoarding: Results of an internet survey. *Behaviour Research and Therapy, 46*(3), 334–344.

Tolin, D.F., Frost, R.O., Steketee, G., Muroff, J. (2015). Cognitive behavioral therapy for hoarding disorder: a meta-analysis. *Depress Anxiety, 2015 Mar;32*(3), 158–66. doi:10.1002/da.22327. Epub 2015 Jan 14. PMID: 25639467.

Tolin, D.F., Levy, H.C., Wootton, B.M., Hallion, L.S. & Stevens, M.C. (2018). Hoarding disorder and difficulties in emotion regulation. *Journal of Obsessive-Compulsive and Related Disorders, 16*, 98–103. https://doi.org/10.1016/j.jocrd.2018.01.006.

Tolin, D.F., Wootton, B.M., Levy, H.C., Hallion, L.S., Worden, B.L., Diefenbach, G.J. & Stevens, M.C. (2019). Efficacy and mediators of a group cognitive–behavioral therapy for hoarding disorder: A randomized trial. *Journal of Consulting and Clinical Psychology, 87*(7), 590.

Tompkins, M.A. (2011). Working with families of people who hoard: A harm reduction approach. *Journal of Clinical Psychology, 67*(5), 497–506.

Turner, K., Steketee, G. & Nauth, L. (2010). Treating elders with compulsive hoarding: A pilot program. *Cognitive and Behavioral Practice, 17*, 449–457.

UK Government. Mental Capacity Act 2005 (c.9) https://www.legislation.gov.uk/ukpga/2005/9/contents

UK Government The Animal Welfare Act 2006 (c. 45) https://www.legislation.gov.uk/ukpga/2006/45

UK Government. Care Act 2014 (c.23) https://www.legislation.gov.uk/ukpga/2014/23/contents/enacted

Williams, B., Harris, P. & Gordon, C. (2020). What is equine hoarding and can 'motivational interviewing' training be implemented to help enable behavioural change in animal owners? *BEVA.* First published: 1 December 2020. https://doi.org/10.1111/eve.13391

Whomsley, S. (2013). The representation of mental health in the media. *Clinical Psychology Forum, 246*, 52–53.

Whomsley S.R.C.(2020). An overview of hoarding difficulties in children and adolescents. *Children Australia, 2020;45(3)*, 182–185. doi:10.1017/cha.2020.29

Wilbram, M., Kellett, S. & Beail, N. (2008). Compulsive hoarding: A qualitative investigation of partner and carer perspectives. *British Journal of Clinical Psychology, 47*, 59–73.

Wincze, J.P., Steketee, G. & Frost, R.O. (2007). Categorization in compulsive hoarding. *Behaviour Research and Therapy, 45*, 63–72.

Woody, S.R., Kellman-McFarlane, K. & Welsted, A. (2014). Review of cognitive performance in hoarding disorder. *Clinical Psychology Review, 34*(4), 324–336.

Yap,K., Timpano, K.R, Isemann, S., Svehla, J. & Grisham, J.R. (2023).High levels of loneliness in people with hoarding disorder. *Journal of Obsessive-Compulsive and Related Disorders, Volume 37, 2023,*100806. https://doi.org/10.1016/j.jocrd.2023.100806.

Zaboski, B.A. Merritt, O.A., Schrack, A.P., Gayle, C., Gonzalez, M., Guerrero, L.A., Dueñas, J.A., Soreni, N. & Mathews, C.A. (2019). Hoarding: A meta-analysis of age of onset. *Depression and Anxiety, 36*(6), 552–564. doi:10.1002/da.22896.

Zerkel, J. (2014). Are you a digital hoarder? Retrieved 20 June 2014 from http://hereandnow.wbur.org/2012/04/12/digital-hoarder-computer.

Resources

Cooke, J. (2017). *Understanding hoarding*. London: Sheldon Press.

Tolin, D., Frost, R.O. & Steketee, G. (2014). *Buried in treasures: Help for compulsive hoarding (2nd edn)*. New York: Oxford University Press.

Singh, S., Hooper, M., Jones, C. (2015). *Overcoming hoarding: A self-help guide using cognitive behavioural techniques*. London: Overcoming books.

Steketee, G. & Frost, R. (2014). *Treatment for hoarding disorder workbook (2nd edn)*. New York: Oxford University Press.

Steketee, G. & Bratiotis, C. (2020). *Hoarding – What everyone needs to know*. Oxford: OUP.

Help for compulsive hoarders and their families: http://www.helpforhoarders.co.uk/.

Resources to assist leading the Buried in Treasures workshop: http://www.ocfoundation.org/uploadedfiles/Hoarding/Help_for_Hoarding/Facilitators

Support for children of hoarders: http://www.childrenofhoarders.com.

Appendix A: DSM-5 diagnostic criteria for hoarding disorder

DSM-5 criteria	Descriptor
Criterion A	Persistent difficulty with discard of objects or possessions, regardless of their actual value.
Criterion B	Difficulties with discard are due to a perceived need to save the possessions and due to the distress created by discard.
Criterion C	Accumulation of clutter that congests living areas and compromises the functioning of the living area.
Criterion D	Presence of clinically significant psychological or emotional distress or impairment to social or work functioning (or any other area).
Criterion E	The hoarding is not attributable to any other medical condition.
Criterion F	The hoarding is not better accounted by the symptoms of another mental health problem.

(APA, 2013)

www.ingramcontent.com/pod-product-compliance
Lightning Source LLC
La Vergne TN
LVHW072051080426
835510LV00029B/3441